ALSO BY SHELDON GLUECK

WAR CRIMINALS

THEIR PROSECUTION AND PUNISHMENT

"Of all the literature on this much-canvassed topic . . . Professor Glueck's book is by far the most complete, learned, interesting and convincing exposition of the subject." *London Law Journal*

"The book is a great scientific achievement and deserves wide reading not only by the jurist but by the layman." *The Nation*

"I think that Professor Glueck's book is of utmost importance and of great public value at this time." *Charles Cheney Hyde*

THIS IS A BORZOI BOOK
published in New York by Alfred A. Knopf

The Nuremberg Trial
AND
Aggressive War

FOREWORD BY

ROBERT H. JACKSON

Justice of the Supreme Court of the United States

———————————

*Chief of Counsel for the United States in prosecuting
the principal Axis War Criminals*

———————————

THE
Nuremberg Trial
AND
Aggressive War

By SHELDON GLUECK

PROFESSOR OF CRIMINAL LAW AND CRIMINOLOGY
AT HARVARD UNIVERSITY

1946 · ALFRED · A · KNOPF · NEW YORK

To BERNARD L. TOUROFF

---

with affectionate regard

FOREWORD

One of the first American penologists and lawyers to draw attention to the need for an inquest into the criminal character of the Nazi war regime was Professor Sheldon Glueck. In 1944 some time before the end of the war, he wrote *War Criminals: Their Prosecution and Punishment* which was a pioneer contribution to this subject. Until his work was published, discussion of the Nazi misdeeds had been largely in terms of political condemnation rather than of legal prosecution.

When negotiations for a Four-Power agreement for the trial of Nazi war criminals began in London in June 1945, Professor Glueck's book was one of the few published studies of the problems involved in trial. When I was appointed as Representative and Chief of Counsel for the United States, he became an Advisor during those negotiations. As captured documents began to pour in, he also devised a system for summarizing and indexing them, so that a large mass of material could be readily available on any particular point. His original plan is substantially the system pursued throughout the Nürnberg trial. Dr. Glueck's study of the basis of criminal liability of the Nazi leaders, therefore, is not the result of merely theoretical knowledge. It is based on practical working acquaintance with the problems which must be faced in the application of the law to the accused.

In the evolution of the law that it is a criminal offense to plan, incite, or wage a war of aggression, or to enter into a combination, common plan, or conspiracy so to do, there are fortunate consequences of its first application to the Nazi criminals of World War II. There are many theoretical difficulties which cause violent debate but which do not plague us practically in the Nürnberg case at all. What is aggression and what is self-defense? These questions might cause considerable trouble in other circumstances. But the evidence at Nürnberg has shown that in this war an aggressive intention was declared by the Nazis— secretly of course—from the very beginning; an intention to get their neighbors' lands without the incumbrance of the neighbors. The evidence has shown a long period of secret preparation for that end, followed by open preparation. Then military force was used as a threat and weapon in diplomacy, which reached its climax at Munich. Then, as Germany's neighbors strengthened in resistance to threats, detailed military plans were prepared for actual attack on Poland. We have the minutes of the secret meetings at which "incidents" were planned as excuses for German attack. We have the proof that border trouble charged to the Poles were in fact perpetrated by Germans provided with Polish uniforms for the occasion. We have the German propaganda films recording with pride their successive invasions and the terrible destruction that followed. The record shows a conquest of Poland in 18 days. When with renewed fury the attack in the West began, Denmark and Norway were overrun in a few days, The Netherlands and Belgium went down in a couple of weeks, the English were driven off the Continent with the memorable disaster of Dunkirk, and in a few days more France fell. Then came the drive into the Balkans and the attack on Russia. In not one of these invasions is it claimed that Germany was actually attacked first, or that any one of these countries, with the possible exception of Russia, had the forces to make attack on Germany a serious threat. Even their aggregate forces were pathetically unequal to the strength built up by purposeful German preparation since the inception of the Nazi regime. Indeed, several of the Nazis on trial have admitted that they felt at that time no menace to Germany from any power.

The result is that by any possible definition of aggression, this war was aggressive in its plotting and execution. It can neither be excused nor justified by any definition of self-defense ever proposed by any responsible authority. The Nürnberg trial, therefore, has avoided wrangles over definitions and deals with the clean-cut challenge—is it a crime to make a war of aggression?

I shall not trespass on Dr. Glueck's field by arguing this point. Whatever the state of law has been, such conduct is a crime now. When representatives of the four nations—the United States, the United Kingdom, Soviet Russia, and France—set their signatures to the Agreement of August 8, 1945 in London, the old order, by which all war was legal, visibly passed away. I think it already had passed away and that the London Agreement only recognized an evolution that already had been consummated. Nineteen nations apart from the signatories have now adhered to that Agreement. It represents the consensus of opinion and judgment among the greater number of civilized nations.

It is true that the London Agreement is more explicit in declaring aggressive war to be a crime than any preceding international document. This may be because greater explicitness was required in a legal document than in a diplomatic undertaking. It may be because the London Agreement represents the work of jurists and lawyers rather than diplomats. In the negotiations the United Kingdom was represented by the Lord Chancellor and the Attorney General; the Provisional Government of France appointed Judge Robert Falco of its highest court, the Cour de Cassation; Soviet Russia sent I. T. Nikitchenko, Vice-President of the Soviet Supreme Court. I represented the President of the United States who, as Commander-in-Chief, participated on behalf of the United States in establishing the International Military Tribunal.

The agreed trial procedure is not that of any one country or system. It embodies several compromises between Continental and Anglo-American proced-ures. The divergent legal philosophies of these coun-tries, however, have been reconciled in a workable procedure which, as I think has been demonstrated, preserves every element of a fair hearing.

The most controversial and fundamental question concerning the trial is the one to which Dr. Glueck has addressed himself. This question—whether it is a crime to conduct a war of aggression—is not technically an issue in the trial itself, having been foreclosed by the specific terms of the London Agreement. How-ever, to those who claim that to hold the Axis leaders criminally responsible for the conduct of a war of aggression is to impose liability *ex post facto* Professor Glueck presents a convincing answer. He argues effectively in support of the proposition that the wag-ing of a war of aggression was criminal even under the International Law which preceded the London Agreement and that that instrument is therefore only declaratory of existent law. Certainly no future lawyer or nation undertaking to prosecute crimes against the peace of the world will have to face the argument that the effort is unprecedented, and therefore, by inference, improper.

To those interested in the legal developments and considerations which underlie the London Agreement of August 8, 1945 and the Nürnberg trial, I commend the scholarly research and persuasive analysis of Dr. Glueck.

ROBERT H. JACKSON
U. S. Chief of Counsel

Nürnberg, Germany,
May 1, 1946.

ACKNOWLEDGMENTS

Thanks are due The Harvard Law Review Association for permission to reproduce my article on "The Nuremberg Trial and Aggressive War," which appeared in Volume 59, No. 3 of the *Harvard Law Review*, February, 1946. I wish also to thank the capable Editors of the *Review* for the great care with which they checked the numerous citations.

S. G.

CONTENTS

The Nuremberg Trial

AND

Aggressive War

CHAPTER I

The Issue

On August 8, 1945, the four major Powers entered into an executive agreement,[1] in which they provided for the establishment of an *ad hoc* International Military Tribunal for the trial of war criminals whose offenses "have no particular geographical location," and, in an Annex to the agreement, set forth a Charter for the "Constitution of the International Military Tribunal."

Article 6, clause (b) of the Charter includes, among the acts to "be considered criminal violations of International Law" and "within the jurisdiction of the Tribunal," the act of *"Launching a war of aggression."* And the indictment which is the basis for the historic prosecution of the Nazi ringleaders at Nuremberg im-

---

[1] "Agreement by the Government of the United States of America, the Provisional Government of the French Republic, the Government of the United Kingdom of Great Britain and Northern Ireland and the Government of The Union of Soviet Socialist Republics for the Prosecution and Punishment of the Major War Criminals of the European Axis" (1945) 13 *U.S. Dept. of State Bull.* 222; *Trial of War Criminals* (Department of State Publication 2420, Washington, 1945) 13 [hereinafter cited as *Trial of War Criminals*].

plements this in "Count Two: Crimes against Peace," the opening paragraph of that charge being as follows:

All the defendants, with divers other persons, during a period of years preceding 8th May 1945, participated in the planning, preparation, initiation and waging of wars of aggression, which were also wars in violation of international treaties, agreements and assurances.[2]

Is there a rational and just basis for this regarding of a war of aggression (*i.e.*, one not clearly justifiable on the ground of self-defense or as an executive act of punishment by the Community of law-abiding States against a law-violating Member) as an international crime? And if the launching of an aggressive war is to be deemed a criminal offense, who is the criminal? The aggressive State? Its responsible (*i.e.*, policy-making) statesmen? Its responsible military leaders, such as members of its General Staff?

During the preparation of my previous book on the subject of war crimes,[3] I was not at all certain that the acts of launching and conducting an aggressive war could be regarded as "international crimes." I

---

[2] *Trial of War Criminals,* p. 39. Count I dealt with "The Common Plan or Conspiracy" to commit "or which involved the commission of, Crimes against Peace, War Crimes, and Crimes against Humanity, as defined in the Charter"; Count III charged the commission of "War Crimes," and Count IV, the commission of "Crimes against Humanity."

[3] *War Criminals: Their Prosecution and Punishment* pp. 37–8, New York: Alfred A. Knopf.

---

finally decided against such a view, largely on the basis of a strict interpretation of the Treaty for the Renunciation of War (Briand-Kellogg Pact), signed in Paris in 1928. I was influenced also by the practical question of policy. Since liability of the leading Nazi malefactors under familiar principles of the laws and customs of war and the Hague and Geneva Conventions was clear, it seemed to be an unnecessary and dangerous complication to resort to prosecution for the "crime" of aggressive war, involving a doctrine open to debate and one which might require long and questionable historical inquiries not suited to judicial proceedings. However, further reflection upon the problem has led me to the conclusion that for the purpose of conceiving aggressive war to be an international crime, the Pact of Paris may, together with other treaties and resolutions, be regarded as evidence of a sufficiently developed *custom* to be acceptable as international law.

Judging from available published data, this idea of including the launching of an aggressive war—a "crime against peace"—among the offenses for which the Axis Powers were to be held liable had its origin, so far as American policy is concerned, in a report to the President made on June 7, 1945, by the American Chief of Counsel for the prosecution of major war criminals. Justice Robert H. Jackson there said:

It is high time that we act on the juridical principle that aggressive war-making is illegal and criminal.[4]

Speaking of the alleged "retroactive" nature of a trial and punishment for the launching of legally prohibited (*i.e.*, aggressive) warfare, Justice Jackson argued:

International Law is more than a scholarly collection of abstract and immutable principles. It is an outgrowth of treaties or agreements between nations and of accepted customs.[5] But every custom has its origin in some single act, and every agreement has to be initiated by the action of some state. Unless we are prepared to abandon every principle of growth for International Law, we cannot deny

[4] Report of June 7, 1945, from Justice Robert H. Jackson, Chief of Counsel for the United States in the prosecution of Axis War Criminals reprinted in (1945) 39 *Am. J. Int. L.* (Supp.) 178, 187; (1945) 12 *U.S. Dept. of State Bull.* 1071, 1077; *Trial of War Criminals,* p. 9. But see Bernays, "Legal Basis of the Nuremberg Trials" (1946) 35 *Survey Graphic* 5–9; Levy, "The Law and Procedure of War Crime Trials" (1943) 37 *Am. Pol. Sci. Rev.* 1052, 1077.

[5] Compare the following: "A major fallacy of the American representatives on the Commission of Responsibilities, as of the German delegates to the Versailles peace conference, was to take it for granted that the characteristics of a fully developed system of law are indispensable to all 'justice according to law.' Lansing and Scott wanted a world legislature and world criminal *legislation* to exist before establishment of a world criminal court. But a court can also enforce the common or unwritten law. . . . As Sir James Stephen points out, 'It is not till a very late stage in its history that law is regarded as a series of commands issued by the sovereign power of the state. Indeed, even in our own time and country that conception of it is gaining ground very slowly. An earlier, and to some extent a still prevailing, view of it is that it is more like an art or science, the principles of which are at first enunciated vaguely, and are gradually

that our own day has its right to institute customs [6] and to conclude agreements that will themselves.become sources of a newer and strengthened International Law. International Law is not capable of development by legislation, for there is no continuously sitting international legislature. Innovations and revisions in International Law are brought about by the action of governments designed to meet a change in circumstances. It grows, as did the common law, through decisions reached from time to time in adapting settled principles to new situations.[7] Hence I am not disturbed by the lack of precedent for the inquiry we propose to conduct.[8]

Nevertheless, the case for prosecuting individuals and States for the "crime" of launching an aggressive war is not as strong as the case for holding them responsible for violations of the recognized laws and customs of legitimate warfare.

---

reduced to precision by their application to particular circumstances. Somehow, no one can say precisely how . . . certain principles came to be accepted as the law of the land.' That branch of the law of nations which deals with prohibited acts of warfare is as yet as undeveloped as was the early English common law." *Glueck op. cit.*, pp. 97–98.

[6] "Much of the law of nations has its roots in custom. Custom must have a beginning; and customary usages of States in the matter of national and personal liability for resort to prohibited methods of warfare and to wholesale criminalism have not been petrified for all time. 'International Law was not crystallized in the seventeenth century, but is a living and expanding code.'" *Id.* at 14.

[7] See note 5.

[8] Report of Chief of Counsel, *supra* note 4 at 187; *Trial of War Criminals*, p. 9.

Is it strong enough to support the relevant count in the Nuremberg indictment?

At the outset it is not amiss to refer to the fact that the United Nations could have executed the Nuremberg defendants without any judicial procedure whatsoever. The "law" of an armistice or a treaty is, in the final analysis, the will of the victor. Although duress may be a good ground for repudiation of an international contract entered into during a period of peaceful relationships between law-observing States, compulsion is to be expected and is an historic fact in the case of international agreements imposed by a victorious belligerent State upon the vanquished. It is frequently claimed that *all* agreements between States must be in conformity with international law; but it must not be forgotten that such inter-State "agreements" as armistices and treaties of peace also *make* international law. In the final analysis, the main considerations which limit the action of a victorious belligerent in imposing an armistice or a treaty of peace are a decent respect for the judgment of history and the fear of later reprisal. One can only recall, in passing, to what extent these considerations played a part in the agreements imposed by the Germans upon the States they vanquished.

The United Nations could, then, have disposed of the Nazi ringleaders summarily by "executive" or "political" action, without any trial at all and without any consideration whatsoever of whether the acts with which the accused were charged had or had not previously been prohibited by some specific provision of international penal law. The exile of Napoleon to Elba, and his subsequent banishment to St. Helena are frequently cited as good illustrations of such non-judicial, or executive, action. By the Convention of April 11, 1814, entered into between Austria, Prussia, Russia, and Napoleon, the latter agreed to retire to Elba. After his escape and re-entry into France with an armed force, the Congress of Vienna, on March 13, 1815, issued a Declaration that by having violated his agreement Napoleon had "destroyed the sole legal title upon which his existence depended, . . . placed himself outside the protection of the law, and manifested to the world that it can have neither peace nor truce with him." The Powers declared that Napoleon had put himself outside "civil and social relations, and that, as Enemy and Perturbator of the World, he has incurred liability to public vengeance." Had the Allies followed the recommendation of the Prussian Field Marshal Blücher, Napoleon would then have been shot on sight as one who, under the above Declaration, was an "outlaw." But after Napoleon's surrender to the British, a Convention was entered into on August 2, 1815, by which Napoleon was "considered by the Powers . . . as their Prisoner," his custody to be "specially entrusted to the British government," the "choice of the Place and of the measures which can best secure the object of the present stipulation" being "reserved to His Britannic Majesty." [9]

Now a political disposal of the case presented by notorious enemies of international law need not be limited to mere imprisonment.[9a] If ever there was a gang of malefactors who deserved extermination without the privilege of legal defense, it is the Nazi ringleaders. Enough reliable information regarding the deliberate mass-murders planned and executed by most of them was at hand to have justified their execution without a formal trial. In his historic address after the sinking of the *Greer*, President Roosevelt correctly called the Nazi ringleaders "international outlaws," [10] just as Napoleon, before his banishment to St. Helena, had been formally declared to be an international outlaw. It would have been poetic justice of the most appropriate kind to have dealt with the Nazi-Fascist ringleaders summarily.

---

[9] *British and Foreign Papers* (1814–15) 665; see also 727 *et seq.; id.* (1815–16) 200 *et seq.;* 56 Geo. III, C.C. 22, 23 (1816). Statesmen of the United Nations have at various times solemnly declared the Nazi leaders to be subject to punishment for their war crimes. See Appendix B.

[9a] As this was going to press, my attention was called to Professor Goodhart's view that "to execute a man without legal trial . . . is closely akin to murder." Goodhart, "The Legality of the Nuremberg Trials," (1946) 58 *Jurid. Rev.*, pp. 1, 18–19.

[10] "Address by the President, September 11, 1941" (1941) 5 *U.S. Dept. of State Bull.* 193, 196.

But the United Nations wished to proceed in a more civilized way. So the victors provided for indictment and trial. They wished to give the accused every reasonable opportunity to disprove, by documents and witnesses, the charges as formally drawn and as supported by an overwhelming mass of evidence. "The victor may justly consider it unwise to disdain the aid which existing law is in a position to offer . . . at the close of a war the essential purpose of which is to vindicate the law of nations." [11] Even notorious criminals caught red-handed ought, in a civilized polity, to be given an opportunity to explain and defend. And, even pirates, who, under the law of nations may be punished by any State capturing them, should, according to modern international law, be given the benefit of a trial if that be feasible.[12] Consequently, Section IV (Art. 16) of the Charter of the International Military Tribunal, which is entitled, "Fair Trial for Defendants," provides for the giving of detailed particulars in the indictment; the furnishing of the indictment and all appurtenant documents, in appropriate translation,

---

[11] Lauterpacht, "The Law of Nations and the Punishment of War Crimes" (1944). *Brit. Y. B. Int.* L. 58.

[12] "In former times it was said to be a customary rule of International Law that pirates could at once after seizure be hanged or drowned by the captor. But this cannot now be upheld, although some writers assert that it is still the law. It would seem that the captor may execute pirates on the spot only when he is not able to bring them safely into a port for trial . . ." Oppenheim, *International Law* (5th ed., Lauterpacht, 1937) 492.

to the accused, the permitting of the defendant, during preliminary examination or trial, to give any relevant explanation of the charges; the translation of the examination and trial proceedings into a language understandable by the accused; the granting to him of the right to conduct his own defense or have the assistance of counsel; and the granting to him of the right to present any evidence in support of his defense and to cross-examine the prosecution's witnesses.[13] When it is remembered that the victors could have shot the Nazi leaders with no trial at all without violating international customary law, it must be conceded that the United Nations are treating the Nazi leaders with high consideration. One recoils from the thought of what the Nuremberg defendants would have done to our leaders had they won the war.

There are, of course, dangers in the subjection of such international outlaws as the Nazi ringleaders to a formal trial; for instance, the attempt to use it, as some have tried, as an international sounding board for a last ditch effort to keep alive Nazi propaganda. Many publicists and lawyers would therefore have preferred the summary execution of the Nuremberg defendants. In fact the most authoritative statement on

---

[13] *Trial of War Criminals,* p. 19. Many of the numerous Allied official pronouncements on the treatment of Axis war criminals after Allied victory employed language suggestive of formal trial and adjudication of guilt rather than summary political disposal of those deemed culpable. See Appendix B.

the fate awaiting war criminals—the Moscow Declaration of October 30, 1943, which was made by the foreign secretaries of the United States, the United Kingdom, and the Soviet Union, "in the interests of the thirty-two United Nations"—hinted that disposition of the Nazi ringleaders might be by executive action; for after promising to return the ordinary offenders to the scenes of their crimes for trial by local courts, it provided that that decision was "without prejudice to the case of German criminals whose offenses have no particular geographical localization, and who will be *punished by joint decision* of the Governments of the Allies." [14] However, it was finally decided to subject them to trial; [15] and this involves the application of international law.

Before considering the question whether the waging of an aggressive war may legitimately be regarded as an international crime, it will be helpful to review certain of the proceedings at the close of World War I.

[14] "It should not be assumed that the procedure of trial will be necessarily adopted." Winston Churchill, Statement of October 4, 1944, *New York Times*, October 5, 1944, p. 4, col. 4.

[15] *Trial of War Criminals*, p. 13.

CHAPTER II

The Briand-Kellogg Pact and Aggressive War

The Commission of Fifteen appointed by the Preliminary Peace Conference at the end of World War I to examine the responsibility for starting that war and for atrocities committed during its conduct went into the question whether "acts which provoked the World War and accompanied its inception," [1] such as the invasion of Luxemburg by the Germans in violation of the Treaty of London of 1867 and their invasion of Belgium in violation of the Treaties of 1839, were criminal. It pointed out that the deliberate breaches of these "contracts made between the high contracting parties to them," [2] which involved "an obligation which is recognized in international law," [3] were the cynical work not of "some outside Power, but [of] one of the

---

[1] "Commission on the Responsibility of the Authors of the War and on Enforcement of Penalties" (1920) 14 *Am. J. Int. L.*, pp. 95, 118.

[2] *Id.* at 119.

[3] *Ibid.*

very Powers which had undertaken not merely to respect [Luxemburg's and Belgium's] neutrality, but to compel its observance by any Power which might attack it." [4] But despite these "culpable acts," despite this "high-handed outrage . . . committed upon international engagements, deliberately, and for a purpose which cannot justify the conduct of those who were responsible," [5] the Commission was "of opinion that no criminal charge can be made against the responsible authorities or individuals [and notably the ex-Kaiser] on the special head of these breaches of neutrality." [6] Nevertheless, concluded the Commission, "the gravity of these gross outrages upon the law of nations and international good faith is such that the Commission thinks they should be the subject of a formal condemnation by the Conference." [7] The Commission gave two reasons for not regarding as *crimes* the treaty-violating acts of aggression, "which the public conscience reproves and which history will condemn:" [8]

First, "by reason of the purely optional character of the institutions at The Hague for the maintenance of peace [International Commission of Inquiry, Mediation and Arbitration] a war of aggression may not be

---

[4] *Ibid.*
[5] *Id.* at 120.
[6] *Ibid.*
[7] *Ibid.*
[8] *Ibid.*

considered as an act directly contrary to positive law, or one which can be successfully brought before a tribunal such as the Commission is authorized to consider under its terms of reference;[9] second, thorough inquiry into the authorship of the war would entail many handicaps of proof, requiring "difficult and complex problems which might be more fitly investigated" by the more leisurely methods of historians and statesmen than by a court.[10] The latter must obviously depend upon recollections of witnesses and must insist upon reasonable celerity of trial and punishment.

But while recoiling from the charge of *crime* and from trial before a court, the Commission nevertheless recommended that "it would be right for the Peace Conference, in a matter so unprecedented, to adopt special measures, and even to create a special organ in order to deal as they deserve with the authors of such acts,"[11] and declared it to be "desirable that, *for the future, penal sanctions* should be provided for such grave outrages against the elementary principles of international law."[12]

However, throughout the quarter-century between the two World Wars nothing so specific was done by

---

[9] *Id.* at 118.
[10] *Ibid.*
[11] *Id.* at 120.
[12] *Ibid.* (Italics supplied.)

the nations of the world to implement the.Commission's recommendation. The treaty for the Renunciation of War (Briand-Kellogg Pact or "Pact of Paris," signed in Paris on August 27, 1928), to which Germany was a Party and, ironically, the first signatory, condemned recourse to war for the solution of international controversies, renounced it as an instrument of national policy, and bound the signatories to seek the settlement of all disputes by pacific means only. But that historic Pact, too, failed to make violations of its terms international crimes punishable either by an international tribunal or by national courts.[13]

An illuminating debate on the meaning of the Briand-Kellogg Pact, especially on the crucial problem of "sanctions" (punishments), occurred at the historic Budapest meeting of the International Law Association in 1934.[14] Fred H. Aldrich referred to an address by Secretary of State Henry L. Stimson in New York in which he had said: "The Briand-Kellogg Pact provides for no sanction of force. It does not require any signatory to intervene with measures of force in case the Pact is violated. Instead, it rests upon

[13] The treaty entered into force on July 24, 1929, with 46 States depositing ratifications or instruments of adhesion and 16 more then signifying their intention to adhere to the treaty.

[14] *International Law Association, Report of the Thirty-Eighth Conference Held at Budapest,* September 6 to 10, 1934 (1945) 1–70.

the sanction of public opinion, which can be made one of the most potent sanctions of the world." [15] The contrast in points of view was most sharply brought out in the following statements by Mr. Reut-Nicolussi and Dr. Jaroslav Žourek, respectively: ". . . When we were in Oxford I pointed out that we have no criminal law in International Law; therefore we cannot adopt the analogy of criminal law by interpreting the Briand-Kellogg Pact, saying that if an action is forbidden by criminal law everybody else has to abstain from aiding the criminal. The contents of the Briand-Kellogg Pact are but a renouncement of war. . . ." On the other hand it was argued: "The first part of the phrase constituting Article I comprises the *condemnation* of recourse to war. The verb, 'to condemn,' in the French as well as the English acceptation of this expression, comprehends a strong moral judgment of disapprobation. From this it is evident that the first part of Article 1 comprises a norm of *international penal law* protecting the public order and the general interest. The violation of this norm must be considered as an *international crime*." [16] A few other authorities have also insisted that the Pact of Paris established aggressive war as an international crime. Thus, Frangulis takes it for granted that "the ratification of the Briand-

---

[15] Stimson, *The Pact of Paris, Three Years of Development* (Department of State, Publication 357, 1932) 7. See also *id.* at 10, 11.

[16] *Report of the Thirty-Eighth Conference, op. cit. supra* at p. 54 (author's translation and italics).

Kellogg Pact has proclaimed war to be a crime and it has been recognized as such by a large number of States. Hence, in our time penal sanctions are possible, although this was not the case in respect to the war of 1914 and its authors." [17] And Scelle claims that legal "doctrine is in general agreement that recourse to a war of aggression constitutes an international crime." [18]

However, the Budapest Articles of Interpretation, drafted by a group of distinguished jurisconsults in the field of international law, do not specifically declare that a violation of the Briand-Kellogg Pact is a crime, although Article 6 provides that "a violating State is liable to pay compensation for all damage caused by a violation of the Pact to any signatory State or to its nationals." [19] The great majority of expressions of contemporary public opinion on the significance of the Pact of Paris were far from regarding it as an international penal statute.[20] Even the framers of the Pact

[17] "Responsables de la Guerre," in 2 *Dictionnaire Diplomatique* (1933) 581, 585 (author's translation).

[18] Scelle, *Précis de Droit des Gens, Deuxième Partie* (1934), 47 (author's translation). See also *Id., Première Partie* (1932), at 65–66. *Cf.* Hassman, *Der Kellogg-Pakt* (1932), 52; *Borah,* Interview, *New York Times,* March 25, 1928, Sec. 3, p. 1, col. 6.

[19] *Report of the Thirty-Eighth Conference, op. cit.,* p. 68.

[20] See Gerould, *Selected Articles on the Pact of Paris* (1929); Dewey, *Outlawry of War,* in 11 Encyc. Soc. Sci. 508–510 (and bibliography therein cited); Mandelstam, *L'Interprétation du Pacte Briand-Kellogg* (1934), pp. 108–13, 122–3, 137, 146–7, 156.

of Paris did not believe its violation to be criminal as well as illegal; and Mr. Kellogg, in the following passage, implies that the historic treaty which bears his name leaves to a State the determination of its own guilt or innocence when charged with a violation of that treaty:

There is nothing in the American draft of an antiwar treaty which restricts or impairs in any way the right of self-defense. That right is inherent in every sovereign state and is implicit in every treaty. Every nation is free at all times and regardless of treaty provisions to defend its territory from attack or invasion, and *it alone is competent to decide* whether circumstances require recourse to war in self-defense. If it has a good case, the world will applaud and not condemn its action.[21]

Mr. Henry L. Stimson, a statesman and lawyer whose opinion is deserving of the highest respect, in 1932 voiced the American conception of the legal effect of the Briand-Kellogg Treaty in these words:

War between nations was renounced by the signatories of the Briand-Kellogg Treaty. This means that it has be-

[21] *Treaty for the Renunciation of War* (Department of State Publication 468, 1933) 57 (italics supplied). It will be noticed that the analogy to the law of self-defense in criminal cases, which has frequently been said to exist, is not sound; for in that field it is the jury and the tribunal, not the accused, which determine whether or not there was legitimate self-defense, while the provision in the Briand-Kellogg Pact left it to the implicated State itself to decide whether or not it had legitimate grounds for a self-defensive resort to war. See Borchard, "The Multilateral Treaty for the Renunciation of War" (1929) 23 *Am. J. Int. L.*, p. 116.

come *illegal* throughout practically the entire world. It is no longer to be the source and subject of rights. It is no longer to be the principle around which the duties, the conduct, and the rights of nations revolve. It is an *illegal thing.* Hereafter when two nations engage in armed conflict either one or both of them must be wrongdoers—violators of this general treaty law. We no longer draw a circle about them and treat them with the punctilios of the duelist's code. Instead, we denounce them as law-breakers. By that very act, we have made obsolete many legal precedents and have given the legal profession the task of re-examining many of its codes and treaties.[22]

But the fact that the contracting Parties to a treaty have agreed to render aggressive war illegal does not necessarily mean that they have decided to make its violation an international crime.[23] Even a multinational contract and one dealing with a subject so vital to the survival of nations as the Briand-Kellogg Pact

[22] Stimson, *op. cit. supra* note 15, at 4–5. Quoted by Jackson in *Trial of War Criminals,* 9–10. *Cf.* Kunz, *Der Kellogg-Pakt* (1929), 9 *Mit. d. deutschen G. f. Völkerrecht,* pp. 75, 83.

[23] Compare the following statement by Mr. Justice Jackson, upon the signing of the Agreement referred to in note 1, p. 3: "Repeatedly, nations have united in abstract declarations that the launching of aggressive war is illegal. They have condemned it by treaty. But now we have the concrete application of these abstractions in a way which ought to make clear to the world that those who lead their nations into aggressive war face individual accountability for such acts." (1945) 13 *U.S. Dept of State Bull.* 227. *Cf.,* Bullard, "Europe and the Kellogg Treaty" in Gerould, *Selected Articles on the Pact of Paris* (1929) 268, 274: "Calling a criminal an 'outlaw' does not do much good unless you have some machinery for arresting him and locking him up."

is not a penal statute; [24] and the remedy for breach of contract does not consist of prosecution and punishment of the guilty party, but rather of obtaining compensation for its breach. In addition to the sanction of a so-called punitive war, and to the economic sanctions provided in the famous Article 16 of the Covenant of the League of Nations, the remedies available under international law for violations of treaties are: publication of the facts with a view of influencing public opinion against the offending belligerent; protest and demand for punishment of individual offenders, sent to the offending belligerent through neutral diplomatic channels; reprisals; post-war recompense. It is a notorious fact, however, that during both World War I and II, such means have proved ineffective in dealing with a militaristic and arrogant Power such as Germany has shown itself to be.

The most effective recourse is, indeed, not at all to be found against recalcitrant States, but rather in the prosecution and punishment of *individuals*—that is, members of a Government and heads of armed forces

---

[24] The *illegality* of aggressive war under the Briand-Kellogg Pact can, however, be used in connection with the technical defense of "justification and excuse," in prosecutions under *municipal* criminal law. Perhaps, through recognition of the uniform provisions found in the domestic-law penal codes of most civilized States as evidence of a general *custom* (a common denominator) accepted as law, it could also be used in prosecution in a tribunal applying international law. See Appendix A.

who have caused their States ruthlessly to trample upon all law in their orgy of aggression and conquest.

Thus we are back to the major question—whether aggressive war can be denominated an international crime—with the additional question, whether individuals comprising the Government or General Staff of an aggressor State may be prosecuted as liable for such crime.

CHAPTER III

Aggressive War as an International Crime

The Charter under which the International Military Tribunal at Nuremberg is supposed to operate gives dogmatically affirmative answers to both of the questions posed in the last chapter. Article 6 provides as follows:

The Tribunal established by the agreement referred to in Article I hereof for the trial and punishment of the major war criminals of the European Axis countries shall have the power to try and punish persons who, acting in the interests of the European Axis countries, whether as individuals or as members of organizations, committed any of the following crimes . . . for which there shall be individual responsibility:

(a) Crimes against peace: Namely, planning, preparation, initiation or waging of a war of aggression, or a war in violation of international treaties, agreements or assurances, or participation in a common plan or conspiracy for the accomplishment of any of the foregoing.[1]

---

[1] *Trial of War Criminals*, p. 16.

And Article 7 of the Charter of the Tribunal provides as follows:

The official position of defendants, whether as heads of state or responsible officials in government departments, shall not be considered as freeing them from responsibility or mitigating punishment.[2]

There is no question but that, as an act of the will of the conqueror, the United Nations had the authority to frame and adopt such a Charter. And it may well be that the Tribunal at Nuremberg will deem itself completely bound by the restrictions above quoted. It is nevertheless valuable to examine the issues involved, for the sake of those lawyers who insist that it is "illegal" and "ex post facto" to regard aggressive war as a crime and to hold individual members of a Government responsible for such a crime; perhaps, also, despite the restrictions of its organic act, the International Military Tribunal will deem itself competent to hear argument on these basic questions and to dispose of them in a written decision for the sake of legal doctrine and precedent.[3]

As to the first question, when one passes in review the numerous expressions of multinational agreement and opinion—to many of which Germany herself was a Party—solemnly promising non-aggression toward neighboring States, condemning aggressive was as an

[2] *Id.* at 17.
[3] See p. 91.

instrument of national policy, and, in several instances, specifically declaring it to be an international crime, one may reasonably conclude that the time has arrived in the life of civilized nations when an international *custom* has developed to hold aggressive war to be an international crime.

It is familiar law in the international field that custom may, in the words of Article 38 of the Statute of the Permanent Court of International Justice, be considered "as evidence of a general practice accepted as law." If, therefore, a reasonable amount of proof can be adduced of a customary recognition among nations in the modern era that aggressive war is a crime, it need not at all be claimed that the violations of the Briand-Kellogg Pact or of any of the other treaties which Germany has chronically treated as "scraps of paper" in themselves constitute international crimes, in order to hold Germany, Japan, and other Axis nations liable for crimes against the Community of States as protected by international law. All that is necessary is to show that during the present century a widespread custom has developed among civilized States to enter into agreements expressive of their solemn conviction that unjustified war is so dangerous a threat to the survival of mankind and mankind's law that it must be branded and treated as criminal.

What is the evidence of this custom and of this conviction?

In addition to the Pact of Paris, the following solemn international pronouncements may be mentioned:

(1) The agreements limiting the nature of the deeds permissible in the extreme event of war, that is, the Hague Conventions of 1899 [4] and 1907 [5] and the Geneva Conventions of 1929 regulating the treatment of prisoners of war [6] and ameliorating the condition of wounded and ill soldiers.[7] Germany and Japan had ratified (with reservations) the 1907 Hague Convention; Italy the 1899 one. Germany and Italy had ratified the Geneva Convention respecting prisoners of war. When the government of the United States expressed its intention to observe that Convention as to both prisoners of war and civilian internees during the recent war, Japan agreed to do likewise.[8] The Hague and Geneva Conventions, to be sure, took for granted the legality of war; but, from motives both of humanitarianism [9] and mutual prudence, they went so far in

---

[4] 2 Malloy, *Treaties* (1910) 2042; 32 *Stat.* 1803. This was superseded by Hague Convention (IV) of 1907 as between those nations that are Parties to the 1907 agreement, but remained in force as between other States.

[5] U.S. Treaty Ser. (1910) No. 539; 36 *Stat.* 2277 (1910).

[6] U.S. Treaty Ser. (1932) No. 846; 47 *Stat.* 2021 (1932).

[7] U.S. Treaty Ser. (1932) No. 847; 47 *Stat.* 2074 (1932).

[8] (1944) 10 *U.S. Dept. of State Bull.* 78.

[9] Care was taken in Hague Convention (IV) to provide that "Until a more complete code of laws of war has been issued, the high contracting Parties deem it expedient to declare that, in cases not included in the Regulations adopted by them, the inhabitants and the belligerents remain under the protection and the rule of the

the direction of limiting the methods of opening hostilities [Hague Convention (III), 1907] and conducting war, as to be signposts on the road toward a growing conviction that aggressive war must somehow be abolished.[10]

(2) The draft of a treaty of mutual assistance sponsored by the League of Nations in 1923, solemnly declared (Article 1) "that aggressive war is an *international crime*," and that the Parties would "undertake that no one of them will be guilty of its commission."[11] About one-half of the 29 States which replied to a submission of the draft treaty wrote in favor of accepting the text. A major objection was that it would be difficult to define what act would comprise "aggression,"[12]

principles of the law of nations, as they result from the usages established among civilized peoples, from the laws of humanity, and the dictates of the public conscience."

[10] It should be pointed out that the provision of rules of humane warfare and treatment of civilians in wartime is not necessarily inconsistent with a belief that aggressive war ought to be altogether abolished; since even if all the nations of the world solemnly agreed never to resort to aggressive war, there would still be the chance of violation of that agreement, in which event the offending nation might or might not aggravate its original criminalism by acts of illegal cruelty in the conduct of an illicit war.

[11] *Records of the Fourth Assembly, Plenary Meetings, League of Nations Official Journal* (Special Supp. No. 13, 1923) 403. (Italics supplied.)

[12] Letter of J. Ramsay MacDonald to Secretary-General, League of Nations, in *Correspondence Between His Majesty's Government and the League of Nations Respecting the Proposed Treaty of Mutual Assistance* (1924), pp. 10–14. Myers, *Origin and Conclusion of The Paris Pact* (1929), p. 13.

rather than doubt as to the criminalism of aggressive war. The United States was unable to adhere because it was not a member of the League.

(3) The preamble to the League of Nations' 1924 Protocol for the Pacific Settlement of International Disputes ("Geneva Protocol"), after "recognizing the solidarity of the members of the international·community," solemnly asserted that "a war of aggression constitutes a violation of this solidarity and an *international crime*." It went on to say that the contracting parties were "desirous of facilitating the complete application of the system provided in the Covenant of the League of Nations for the pacific settlement of disputes between the States and of ensuring the repression of *international crimes*." [13] The meticulously drafted Geneva Protocol was prepared after years of labor by some of the most distinguished and learned jurists and statesmen. It was warmly welcomed and earnestly recommended to the Members of the League of Nations by a resolution unanimously passed in the Assembly by the vote of forty-five Members of the League (including Italy and Japan—Germany was not as yet a Member), and signed by the representatives of many countries.[14] Not only did it definitely declare

[13] *Records of the Fifth Assembly, League of Nations Official Journal* (Special Supp. No. 23, 1924) 498. (Italics supplied.)

[14] *Id.* at 497. Although the Protocol was not ratified, this fact does not destroy the validity of the argument in the text. The signature of the Protocol by the leading statesmen of the world, representing

aggressive war to be an international crime, but by Article 6 it provided that the sanctions of Article 16 of the Covenant of the League should be applicable to a State resorting to war in disregard of its undertakings under the Protocol. Although it never legally came into force (not, however, because of any serious doubt that a war of aggression could be regarded as an international crime [15]), the historic Protocol of Geneva did express the strong attitude of leading jurists and statesmen of most of the nations of the world regarding both the illegality and the criminalism of aggressive war.[16]

(4) At the eighteenth plenary meeting of the Assembly of the League of Nations, September 24, 1927, all the delegations (including the German, Italian, and Japanese) having pronounced in favor of a Resolution of the Third Committee comprising a Declaration Concerning Wars of Aggression, the Declaration was

the vast majority of civilized States and peoples, is itself evidence of a strongly entrenched custom to regard aggressive war as an international crime.

[15] See Myers, *op. cit.*, for Great Britain's reasons for declining to accept the Protocol. The Geneva Protocol was to some extent superseded by the General Act for the Pacific Settlement of International Disputes, adopted at Geneva, September 26, 1928, to which many States adhered. See 4 Hudson (Ed.) International Legislation (1932), p. 2529.

[16] See the debates, *League of Nations Official Journal* (Special Supp. No. 23, 1924), p. 19, *et seq.;* the *Report of the First and Third Committees, id.,* at 479–97; Miller, *The Geneva Protocol* (1925), p. 112; Schücking, *Das Genfer Protokoll* (1924), p. 5.

declared to be unanimously adopted.[17] Both the eloquent addresses in support of this Declaration [18] and the preamble to the Declaration show how strong was the conviction that the time had arrived, in the affairs of States and their peoples, to call a spade a spade:

The Assembly,
Recognising the solidarity which unites the community of nations;
Being inspired by a firm desire for the maintenance of general peace;
Being convinced that a war of aggression can never serve as a means of settling international disputes and is, in consequence, an *international crime.* . . .[19]

(5) The unanimous Resolution (February 18, 1928) of the twenty-one American Republics at the Sixth (Havana) Pan-American Conference, declared that "war of aggression constitutes an *international crime against the human species.*" [20]

(6) At the International Conference of American States on Conciliation and Arbitration, assembled in

---

[17] *Records of the Eighth Ordinary Session of the Assembly, League of Nations Official Journal* (Special Supp. No. 54, 1927), pp. 155–56.

[18] *Id.* at 82 *et seq.*

[19] *Id.* at 155.

[20] Quoted in *Papers Relating to Foreign Relations of the United States* (Department of State Publication, 1839, 1928), p. 13; (italics supplied).

Washington in December, 1928, representatives of all twenty republics at the Conference signed a General Convention of Inter-American Conciliation, of which the preamble contains the statement, "Desiring to demonstrate that the *condemnation of war* as an instrument of national policy in their mutual relations" set forth in the Havana Resolution, "constitutes one of the fundamental bases of inter-American relations. . . ." [21]

(7) The Anti-War Treaty of Non-Aggression and Conciliation signed at Rio de Janeiro, October 10, 1933, was ratified by 25 States, including the United States of America. The preamble to that treaty states that the Parties were entering into the agreement "to the end of *condemning wars of aggression* and territorial acquisitions that may be obtained by armed conquest, making them impossible and establishing their *invalidity*." [22]

(8) Article 1 of the notable Draft Treaty of Disarmament and Security Prepared by an American Group and carefully considered by the Third Committee (on disarmament) of the Assembly of the

---

[21] (1929) 63 *Bulletin of the Pan American Union* 114.

[22] 4 *Treaties, Conventions, International Acts, Protocols, and Agreements Between the United States and Other Powers* 4793 [Sen. Doc. No. 134, 75th Cong., 3d Sess. (1938)]. One might also mention the numerous treaties of "mutual guarantee," such as the Treaty of Locarno of October 16, 1925, and the treaties entered into by Germany with her neighbors shortly preceding her planned attack on them. See note 11, p. 80.

League of Nations, 1924, provides that "The High Contracting Parties solemnly declare that aggressive war is an *international crime*," and "severally undertake not to be *guilty* of its commission," while Article 2 provides that "A State engaging in war for other than purposes of defence commits the *international crime* described in Article 1." [23]

(9) Finally, the authoritative expression of American opinion on aggressive war was made on December 12, 1927, when Senator William E. Borah introduced a resolution, the last in a long series since 1922, of which a pertinent provision was "that it is the view of the Senate of the United States that war between nations should be outlawed as an institution or means of the settlement of international controversies by making it *a public crime under the law of nations*." [24] One could also mention the views of other distinguished statesmen in support or interpretation of some of the foregoing international pronouncements, which regard aggressive war as a crime. To cite but one, that of Senator Arthur Capper (especially significant since it came from a Republican statesman from the isola-

---

[23] *Records of the Fifth Assembly, Meetings of the Committees, Minutes of the Third Committee, League of Nations Official Journal* (Special Supp. No. 26, 1924) Annex 4, p. 169. (Italics supplied.) This draft also made a notable contribution to the definition of acts of aggression. See also Trainin, *Hitlerite Responsibility under Criminal Law* (trans. Rothstein, 1945), pp. 30–31.

[24] Sen. Res. No. 45, 70th Cong., 1st Sess. (1927); (italics supplied).

tionist Middle West) in commenting upon his resolution in favor of the efforts of Briand which led to the Pact of Paris: "There is every reason to consider this proposal for civilized nations to renounce war as an instrument of public policy, a logical and necessary step toward peace. It goes farther, it seems to me, than merely declaring war *criminal*.[25]

All these solemn expressions of the conviction of civilized States and statesmen regarding the need for conciliation, for the settlement of international disputes by pacific means only, for the renunciation of war as an instrument of national policy, and, logically, for the recognition that aggressive war is an international crime, greatly re-enforce whatever inference to that effect is derivable from the Briand-Kellogg Pact itself. They may be regarded as powerful evidence of the existence of a widely prevalent custom among civilized peoples sufficient to energize a juristic climate favorable to the regarding of a war of aggression as not simply "unjust" or "illegal" but downright *criminal*.

Prevalent custom may legitimately be regarded as a source of international law. As Sir Frederick Pollock long ago pointed out:

Where an agreement or declaration is made not by two or three states as a matter of private business between

[25] Shotwell, *War as an Instrument of National Policy* (1929), p. 97; (italics supplied).

themselves, but by a considerable proportion, in number and power, of civilized states at large, for the regulation of matters of general and permanent interest . . . when all or most of the great Powers have deliberately agreed to certain rules of general application, the rules approved by them have very great weight in practice even among states which have never expressly consented to them. It is hardly too much to say that declarations of this kind may be expected, in the absence of prompt and effective dissent by some Power of the first rank, to become part of the universally received law of nations within a moderate time. As among men, so among nations, the opinions and usage of the leading members in a community tend to form an authoritative example for the whole. . . . It is quite possible that some of the recommendations recorded at the Peace Conference at the Hague in 1899 [and in 1907] may sooner or later . . . be adopted as part of the public law of civilized nations by general recognition *without any formal ratification.*

On the whole, then, the law of nations rests on a general consent which, though it may be supplemented, influenced, and to some extent defined, by express convention, can never be completely formulated under existing conditions. This is as much as to say that the law of nations must be classed with *customary law.*[26]

The validity of custom as a source of international law is a matter not new to the Germans. German authorities have gone so far as to say that the "customs of war [part of international law] are substantive penal

[26] Pollock, *The Sources of International Law* (1902) 2 *Col. L. Rev.* 511, 512 (italics supplied).

law as good as the State's penal legislation"; [27] and that the fact that a State has not previously enacted a penal code setting forth detailed definitions and prescribing various punishments is irrelevant, since it can legitimately resort to enforcement of the customs of war as part of the common law of nations.[28]

The prosecution at Nuremberg under Count Two of the historic indictment, "Crimes Against Peace," for the crimes of "planning, preparation, initiation and waging wars of aggression, which were also in violation of international treaties, agreements and assurances," [29] is, then, strictly speaking, not based upon proof of the breach of any specific provision of any particular one or more of the above-mentioned international treaties or conventions. It is rather based upon violation of customary international law—a system of law that is as obviously subject to growth as has been the law of any other developing legal order, by the crystallization of generally prevailing opinion and practice into law under the impact of common consent and the demands of general world security. Acquiescence of all members of the Family of Nations is not

27 8 Schätzel, *Bestrafungen nach Kriegsbrauch, Archiv für Militärrecht* (1920), pp. 13–24.

28 Verdross, *Die Völkerrechtswidrige Kriegshandlung und der Strafanspruch der Staaten* (1920), pp. 30–32.

29 *Trial of War Criminals,* p. 37. Trainin, *op. cit.,* note 23, at 33, aptly defines international crime as "an infringement of the foundations of international communion."

necessary for this purpose.[30] All that is needed is reasonable proof of the existence of a widespread custom; and the numerous multilateral anti-war treaties, agreements and resolutions, as well as the statements and writings of experts in connection with such international pronouncements, comprise such proof. Obviously, a requirement of unanimity would permit the most lawless State to prevent the recognition of the custom as evidence of the existence of the principle of law.

It is true that among the tests of legally acceptable custom usual in English courts has been the requirement of very long if not "immemorial" usage.[31] But such a requirement developed during a period in world history when the tempo of life was very slow. It is no exaggeration to say that more relevant opinion

[30] "Rules of customary law have had their origin in the practice of a single state or of a group of states; then in time other states have been led from various motives to adopt the same practice until a well-defined usage has grown up, which in its turn has slowly hardened into fixed custom carrying with it a recognition that the practice is no longer voluntary but of obligation. In a broad view, customary law may be regarded as embracing the evolution of general principles as well as the growth of detailed rules from the common practice of states." Fenwick, *International Law* (2d ed. 1934), pp. 62–63. "A custom, in the intendment of law, is such a usage as hath obtained the force of law, and is in truth a binding law to such particular places, persons and things which it concerns. . . . But it is *ius non scriptum*. . . . Viner, *Abr.* vii, 164, citing *Tanistry Case,* Dav. 31 b." Cited by Allen, *Law in the Making* (1927), p. 28, n.1.

[31] *Id.* at 89; see also *id.*, Appendix B, "Reasonableness of Custom," pp. 359–77.

and custom recognizing the dangers of aggressive war and the need of its suppression by all means have been crowded into the short compass of the first half of the twentieth century than in the entire preceding period of recorded history. One has only to think of the tremendous technologic development of the present epoch, with its immense multiplication of dangers to the very survival of mankind, to recognize that for the legal recognition of custom the content of the years, rather than their mere duration, is of prime importance. Moreover, the English test for the acceptability of custom as law developed in areas of private rights and duties which, being in the domain of municipal law, had slowly grown over a long period of time. But systematic international law pertaining to war, its conduct, obligations, rights, and abolition is of relatively recent development; and the time-requirement for the legal validity of custom in that field must, correspondingly, be telescoped.

The claim that in the absence of a specific, detailed, pre-existing *code* of international penal law to which all States have previously subscribed, prosecution for the international crime of aggressive war is necessarily ex post facto because no world legislature has previously spoken is specious. At the close of World War I, in arguing against the application of the common law of nations to individuals, the American representatives on the Versailles Commission (Robert Lansing and James Brown Scott) insisted upon the applicability to the present problem of the reasoning in "the leading case of *United States v. Hudson* (7 Cranch, 32), decided by the Supreme Court of the United States in 1812, that 'the legislative authority of the Union must first make an act a crime, affix a punishment to it, and declare the court that shall have jurisdiction of the offense.' " [32] The American commissioners argued that "what is true of the American States must be true of this looser union which we call the Society of Nations." [33] But this is a *non sequitur*. In the Hudson case a tribunal of a special federation of states was interpreting a specific written constitution in which powers are distributed between the United States of America and the individual states of the Union. But for an historic accident, the case might well have been decided the other way.[34] It is highly questionable

---

[32] "Commission on the Responsibility of the Authors of the War and on Enforcement of Penalties" (1920) 14 *Am. J. Int. L.* 145–46.

[33] *Id.* at 146.

[34] The case arose under the Federal Judiciary Act of 1789, c. 20, §§ 9, 11, giving the Federal courts jurisdiction of all "crimes and offenses cognizable under the authority of the United States." The original draft of this Act which was submitted to Congress gave those courts jurisdiction of all "crimes and offenses cognizable under the authority of the United States *and defined by the laws of the same*," but the last eight words of the draft were not approved by Congress and did not therefore appear in the statute. The implication is that by striking them Congress showed that it did not intend to limit the jurisdiction of the Federal courts to offenses defined by

whether the Hudson case—confined to a local eighteenth century constitutional arrangement within a single nation, and involving the Supreme Court's failure to consult the Senate files for the original draft of the Federal Judiciary Act of 1789—is at all relevant to the issue whether an International Criminal Court established by the majority of civilized States in 1919 or 1945 could or could not legitimately apply the common law of nations to individuals without some world "legislative authority" having first enacted an international penal statute, made its violations crimes, and affixed a specific punishment to each crime.

In the international field, then, as in the domestic, part of the system of prohibitions implemented by penal sanctions consists of customary or common law. In assuming that an act of aggressive war is not merely lawless but also criminal, the Nuremberg court would merely be following the age-old precedent of courts

statute. This significant change in the bill was not known until Charles Warren discovered the original draft in the archives of the United States some twenty years ago. "Had the Supreme Court consulted these Senate Files, it is probable that the decisions in *United States* v. *Hudson*, in 1812, and *United States* v. *Coolidge*, in 1816, might have been otherwise than they were." Warren, *New Light on the History of the Federal Judiciary Act of 1789* (1923) 37 Harv. L. Rev. 49, 51, 73. It should also be borne in mind that Madison was President of the United States from 1809 to 1817 and the Jeffersonian party to which he belonged did not wish to enlarge the powers of the Federal Government more than was necessary. See also I Bishop, *Criminal Law* (9th ed. 1923) 129–32.

which enforce not only the specific published provisions of a systematic code enacted by a legislature,
but also "unwritten" law. During the early stage (or
particularly disturbed stages) of any system of law—
and international law is still in a relatively undeveloped state—the courts must rely a great deal upon
non-legislative law,[35] and thereby run the risk of an
accusation that they are indulging in legislation under
the guise of decision, and are doing so ex post facto.
There is, indeed, a school of juristic thought which perhaps lets too much of the cat out of the bag, in insisting
that courts *usually* indulge in ex post facto reasoning
and decision: "And this brings us to the reason why
courts and jurists have so struggled to maintain the
pre-existence of the Law, why the common run of
writers speak of the judges as merely stating the Law,
and why Mr. Carter, in an advance towards the truth,

---

[35] *"Legislative power comparatively late:* In that centralisation
of different powers included in the modern idea of Sovereignty, the
most important, according to general opinion, of the functions referred to—the Legislative—is, in all probability, one of the latest.
. . . The Judge and the law may follow the Chief, but certainly
come before the King: the Lawgiver comes last of all." Clark, *History of Roman Private Law* (1919) (Part III Regal Period) 388–89.
"Particularly the very notion itself of an oral, unwritten law, de-
livered down from age to age by custom and tradition merely, seems
derived from the practice of the Druids, who never committed any
of their instructions to writing, possibly for want of letters. . . ."
4 Blackstone, *Commentaries* *408. See also 2 Montesquieu, *The
Spirit of the Laws* (3d ed. 1758, trans. by Nugent) pp. 251–52;
Maine, *Ancient Law* (1st ed., 1861) pp. 8, 13, 370–74; Huebner, *A
History of Germanic Private Law* (1918) pp. 5–6.

says of the judges that they are discoverers of the Law. That reason is the unwillingness to recognize the fact that the courts, with the consent of the State, have been constantly in the practice of applying in the decision of controversies, rules which were not in existence and were, therefore, not knowable by the parties when the causes of controversy occurred. It is the unwillingness to face the certain fact that courts are constantly making *ex-post facto* Law." [36] And a distinguished English authority, Lord Wright, reminds us that:

It is just by the proper use of elasticity in the authorities that the law is advanced. If that were not so, the law could never have changed. How otherwise explain the difference between the law of tort, or of trusts, or of the sale of goods as it was a hundred years ago and as it is now? In these matters statutory changes have on the whole been of minor importance, yet the law might almost be regarded as a new and different law, were it not that we can trace the development from point to point, as the judges found the requirements of justice compelled them to modify or vary or innovate on the law, creating new or partially new principles, but keeping, actually or ostensibly, within or close to the decided cases. This, apart from the decision of matters of fact, is the great work of the English judges. There was reposed on them the great responsibility of making the law, which on the whole they have worthily fulfilled.[37]

[36] Gray, *The Nature and Sources of the Law* (2d ed. 1921) pp. 99–100; see also *id.* at 231–32.

[37] Lord Wright, "The Common Law in Its Old Home," in *The Future of the Common Law* (1937) p. 79.

In England, even the most serious offenses (e.g., murder, manslaughter, robbery, rape, arson, mayhem) originated as crimes by way of custom. From the earliest times of legal development, both before and after prosecution in the royal courts for violation of the "King's peace" had taken the place of the ancient practices of private vengeance, the wergild, and trial by ordeal, such customary crimes were recognized; and when the King's courts took over, they accepted common law crimes as part of "the custom of the realm," without specific prior statute or royal decree. Even later,

"from 1660 to 1860, the courts, without any specific precedent, frequently punished conduct which was *contra bonos mores,* or which openly outraged public decency, or which was subsumable under some similar generalization; and there are scattered instances of the courts having continued this practice after 1860." [38]

[38] Hall, "Nulla Poena Sine Lege" (1937) 47 *Yale L. J.* 165, 179. It should be pointed out that the consequences of conviction for these common-law offenses were serious in a period of severe penalties during which the magistrates might "punish the offenders by fine, imprisonment, and such other corporal punishment as the circumstances may require," for such offenses as "contempt of the established religion" or "open breaches of morality exhibited in the face of the people," which offenses tend to breaches of the peace or "sap public morals." 1 East, *Pleas of the Crown* (2d ed. 1803), c. 1, § 1. See also *id.* c. 4, § 10 (counterfeiting foreign coin). Evidently, also, the non-statutory offense of "delay in discovering high treason, whatever excuses the party might have for it, was deemed an assent to it, and consequently high treason," and therefore punishable capitally. Hawkins, *Pleas of the Crown* (8th ed. 1824) c. 5, § 2.

Now whenever an English common-law court for the first time held that some act not previously declared by Parliament to be a crime was a punishable offense for which the doer of that act was now prosecuted and held liable, or whenever a court, for the first time, more specifically than theretofore defined the constituents of a crime and applied that definition to a new case,[39] the court in one sense "made law." Yet, fundamentally, it thereby did no violence to the technique of law-enforcement or the requirements of man-made justice, unless it acted most unreasonably and arbitrarily. Even the legal "command" which, since Austin's time is deemed by many to be the indispensable and distinctive hallmark of law, was essentially present. It is true that the command which the accused was held to have violated did not come directly and specifically from the legislature or sovereign; but since the prohibition represented the consensus of the people as reflected in customary usage, it contained enough of the imperative element to warn

---

[39] "So far as I have been able to discover, there are hardly any definitions of crimes in the early [Anglo-Saxon] laws. . . . Of offenses against property, theft is the one most commonly referred to. I have found no definition of it in any of the laws, though I think it may be said to be the subject to which they refer most frequently. . . . Robbery, *roberia,* is frequently mentioned; but I think no definition of it is given. . . . Of mischievous offenses against property *bernet* or arson is several times mentioned, but with no detail." 1 Stephen, *A History of the Criminal Law of England* (1883), pp. 53, 56–57.

its prospective violators, to impel judges to recognize it as an existing part of the law of the land, and to hold its infringers guilty of a crime.

So is it with modern international common law, in prohibiting aggressive war on pain of punishment. Every custom and every recognition of custom as evidence of law must have a beginning some time; and there has never been a more justifiable stage in the history of international law than the present, to recognize that by the common consent of civilized nations as expressed in numerous solemn agreements and public pronouncements the instituting or waging of an aggressive war is an international crime..

CHAPTER IV

Acts of State

Assuming modern aggressive war to be a crime, i.e., an offense against the Family of Nations and its international law, then the defendant must normally be the implicated State. A familiar analogy is the prosecution of a business corporation. In both cases, of course, the punishment upon conviction can only be in terms of a fine or deprivation of certain rights or privileges. But, as experience has shown, action against a State must necessarily be ineffective in reducing international criminalism, compared to the imposition of penal sanctions upon members of a cabinet, heads of a general staff, or other persons in authority in a Government who have led a State into aggressive war and the breach of basic treaties designed for the security of all States.

As indicated, Article 6 of the Charter of the International Military Tribunal recognizes this fact. By implication, also, Article I of the Agreement for the Establishment of an International Military Tribunal, of which the Charter is an integral part, provides for personal rather than State liability:

There shall be established after consultation with the Control Council for Germany an International Military Tribunal for the trial of war criminals whose offenses have no particular geographical location whether they be accused *individually* or in their capacity as members of organizations or groups or in both capacities.[1]

So also, the numerous solemn warnings to the Axis leaders by statesmen of the chief Member-States of the United Nations during the conduct of the war implied a plan to hold them personally responsible for their crimes.[2]

These were all manifestations of the power of the victor, which could be the sole "law" to govern the treatment of the Nazi ringleaders. But assuming the application of normal legal principles, conservative international lawyers and publicists have pointed to two fundamental obstacles to the prosecution and punishment of the Nazi leaders for the crime of waging a war of aggression; namely, the doctrine of "acts of State," and the related principle that international law obligates and binds only States, not individual human beings.

Taking up the first objection, it is argued that international law forbids a State to make a subject of another State responsible for an act committed by him upon direction or with approval and ratification of

[1] *Trial of War Criminals,* p. 14 (italics supplied). This followed the formula of the Moscow Declaration of November 1, 1943.

[2] See Appendix B.

his State,[3] even if that act is a flagrant war crime and as such clearly contrary to international law itself. Responsibility for such a breach, it is claimed, rests not on the individual, who acted as a mere instrument or "organ" of his State, but only upon the "collectivity of individuals," the corporate entity, which comprises the State. The reason assigned for this principle is that since the act of the individual must be "imputed" to the State, "prosecution of an individual by courts of the injured State for an act which, according to international law, is the act of another State, amounts to exercising jurisdiction over another State; and this is a violation of the rule of general international law that no State is subject to the jurisdiction of another State."[4] It is, moreover, claimed that "there is no sufficient reason to assume that the rule of general customary law under which no State can claim jurisdiction over the acts of another State is suspended by the outbreak of war, and consequently that it is not applicable to the relationship between belligerents."[5]

This argument must be met if the act-of-State doctrine is not, in the minds of certain lawyers, to render

---

[3] Kelsen, "Collective and Individual Responsibility in International Law with Particular Regard to the Punishment of War Criminals" (1943) 31 *Calif. L. Rev.* 530, 539–41. See also Professor Kelsen's *Peace Through Law* (1944).

[4] Kelsen, *supra* note 3, at 540.

[5] *Id.* at 542.

all prosecution of the Nazi ringleaders "illegal" and in the nature of "lynch law."

It may be admitted that there are sound reasons for the familiar application of the act-of-State doctrine to the normal, peaceful intercourse of nations,[6] without it necessarily following that it is also to be applied to the situation presented by the acts of the Nazi ringleaders in instituting a criminal war and conducting it barbarously. However, the American members of the Commission on Responsibility which was set up by the Peace Conference at Versailles in 1919, in their Memorandum of Reservations (April 4, 1919), insisted upon the applicability of the act-of-State argument to the plan to try the former German Kaiser. They relied upon "the masterly and hitherto unanswered opinion of Chief Justice Marshall, in the case of the *Schooner Exchange* v. *McFaddon and Others* (7 Cranch 116), decided by the Supreme Court of the United States in 1812, in which the reasons are given for the exemption of the sovereign and of

---

[6] *E.g.*, to prevent interference by the domestic courts of one State with the conduct of the affairs of a friendly foreign State within that State's own borders, thus imperiling friendly relations: "To permit the validity of the acts of one sovereign State to be reëxamined and perhaps condemned by the courts of another would very certainly 'imperil the amicable relations between governments and vex the peace of nations.'" *Oetjen* v. *Central Leather Co.*, 246 U.S. 297, 304 (1918); see also *Underhill* v. *Hernandez*, 168 U.S. 250, 252 (1897); 2 Montesquieu, *The Spirit of the Laws* (3d ed. 1758, trans. by Nugent), c. 21.

the *sovereign agent of a state* from judicial process."[7] But that classic decision (as Chief Justice Marshall was careful to point out) dealt with the normal, peacetime relations of friendly sovereigns. The immunity which a sovereign and his agents enjoy by virtue of the privilege granted him and them by other sovereigns is based upon international comity and courtesy; and its recognition is dependent upon an important condition precedent: that the sovereign in question, or his agent, be conducting himself in conformity with international law.[8] The host sovereign can otherwise refuse to grant immunity. Starting with the proposition that "all sovereigns have consented to a relaxation, in practice, in cases under certain peculiar circumstances, of that absolute and complete jurisdiction within their respective territories which sovereignty confers,"[9] Marshall recognized a class of cases "in which every sovereign is understood to waive the exercise of a part of that complete exclusive territorial jurisdiction, which has been stated to be the at-

---

[7] (1920) 14 *Am. J. Int. L.* 135 (italics supplied). See Appendix C, for the facts in this historic case.

[8] "International law . . . speaking very generally . . . recognizes that every state has, as a sovereign community, the legal right to select its own form of government and to regulate as it chooses its own territory and the personal and property relations of its citizens and subjects—*in so far as it does not exercise this right in such ways as to endanger the peace and safety of other states.*" Coker, "Sovereignty" in 14 *Encyc. Soc. Sci.* (1937) 266 (italics supplied).

[9] 7 Cranch 116, 136 (1812).

tribute.of every nation. . . . One of these is admitted to be the exemption of the person of the sovereign [or his agent] from arrest or detention within a foreign territory." [10] But he went on to say that: ". . . all exemptions from territorial jurisdiction, must be derived from the consent of the sovereign of the territory; . . . this consent may be implied or expressed; and . . . when implied, its extent must be regulated by the nature of the case, and the views under which the parties requiring and conceding it must be supposed to act." [11] Thus, while holding it to be "a principle of public law, that national ships of war, entering the port of a friendly power, open for their reception, are to be considered as exempted by the consent of that power from its jurisdiction," [12] the court was careful to point out that "without doubt, the sovereign of the place is capable of destroying this implication." [13]

Surely, it cannot reasonably be argued that the license in question, which is dependent upon the consent of sovereigns and therefore upon the existence of friendly relations between the States involved and upon the lawful behavior of the sovereign who seeks immunity from extraterritorial jurisdiction for himself or his agents, is applicable to the situation of the Nazi

[10] *Id.* at 137.
[11] *Id.* at 143.
[12] *Id.* at 145.
[13] *Id.* at 145, 146.

ringleaders. Surely, it is more reasonable to assume
that by invading neighboring countries in flagrant violation of treaty obligations and for purposes of aggression, conquest and the mass-extermination of the
subjects of neighboring States, an offending sovereign
destroys any implied consent that he be exempt from
the jurisdiction of others, and strips himself and his
agents of any mantle of immunity he may have claimed
by virtue of international comity.

An issue of this kind ought not to be disposed of on
the basis of blind legalistic conceptualism; it should
be dealt with realistically in the light of the practical
as well as logical results to which one or the other
solution will lead. An examination of the act-of-State
doctrine from such a point of view shows it to be so
unreasonable and dangerous to law-abiding peoples
as to cast grave doubt on the question whether it ever
was sound law.

Wharton, commenting on *People* v. *McLeod*,[14] and
the historic debate between Webster and Calhoun on
the question of the liability of a foreign national for
crimes committed by order of his State on American
soil, pointed out that: "To admit to its full extent the
principle that we cannot subject to our municipal laws
aliens who violate such laws under direction of their
sovereigns, would be to give such sovereigns jurisdic-

---

[14] 25 *Wend.* 481 (N.Y. 1841). See Appendix D for the facts in
this significant case.

tion over our soil." [15] From this it must follow that a sovereign's agent will *not* be exempt from liability, if his act is not justifiable under international law.

Moreover, as Marshall implied, even in an age when the doctrine of sovereignty had a strong hold,[16] the non-liability of agents of a State for "acts of State" must rationally be based upon an assumption that no member of the Family of Nations will order its agents to commit flagrant violations of international and criminal law. It must rather rest upon an assumption that a State will prohibit its own subjects from committing acts of defiance of law so grave as to endanger

---

[15] I Wharton, *A Digest of the International Law of the United States* (1886) 67. See Glueck, *op. cit.*, pp. 230–32.

[16] Those statesmen and lawyers who have raised the concept of "Sovereignty" to the status of some holy fetish have ignored historical facts. The more rigid, legalistic notions of sovereignty are of comparatively late (nineteenth-century) origin or rebirth. "As in the sixteenth century, so again in the nineteenth century practical political considerations influenced the precise formulation of a theory that attributed to a definite sovereign an authority unrestrained by law." Coker *supra* note 8, at 265, 267 (and authorities therein cited). Practical considerations in our era, such as the fact that sovereigns of certain nations have several times clearly demonstrated their self-appointed divine right to trample over the territory and lives of neighboring peoples in violation of solemn treaty obligations, and particularly the sobering fact of the advent of the atomic bomb, should bring about a reformulation of the theory of national sovereignty. It is to be noted that the basis of sovereign immunity in the field of civil liability has, partly under the impact of the facts of modern technology and the modifications in culture thereby brought about, been breaking down. See Angell, "Sovereign Immunity—the Modern Trend" (1925) 35 *Yale L. J.* 150.

the peace and security of other States, as well as its own, and, far from condoning such acts, will punish them. As Blackstone long ago pointed out:

> . . . where the individuals of any state violate this general [i.e., international] law, it is then the interest as well as duty of the government under which they live to animadvert upon them with a becoming severity that the peace of the world may be maintained. For in vain would nations in their collective capacity observe these universal rules, if private subjects were at liberty to break them at their own discretion, and involve the two states in a war. It is therefore incumbent upon the nation injured, first, to demand satisfaction and justice to be done on the offender by the state to which he belongs; and, if that be refused or neglected, *the sovereign then avows himself an accomplice or abettor of his subject's crime, and draws upon his community the calamities of foreign war.*[17]

Blackstone assumed that a sovereign would not willingly ally himself with the criminal acts of his agents. But where a State clearly sets out to put into effect its own calculated plan of criminally aggressive warfare, mass-murder, and mass-pillage it is absurd to believe that it will disclaim the crimes of its agents in carrying out its plan, or will punish them if left to its own

---

[17] Blackstone, *Commentaries* *68 (italics supplied). How much more civilized it is if, instead of the sovereign accomplice drawing "upon his community the calamities of foreign war," he and the other planners and executors of a war in violation of solemn treaty obligations are subjected to the civilized methods of prosecution and trial and, if convicted, to individual punishment.

devices. The whole sorry mess of the trial of German war criminals after the World War I in the German Supreme Court at Leipzig tends to demonstrate this. The 896 serious offenders submitted for prosecution on the Allied list, were soon cut down to a "test" list of only 45. The number actually tried was only twelve; the number convicted, six. The sentences were for imprisonment only, and that usually for absurdly brief periods of months; and the two convicts sentenced for U-boat atrocities soon escaped, with what appears to have been official connivance. A German general, clearly guilty of ordering the massacre of wounded prisoners of war, was found not guilty despite abundant proof; and his acquittal was greeted with applause and flowers by the Germans attending the trial.[18]

It could very reasonably be argued, moreover, that in modern times a State is—*ex hypothesi*—incapable of ordering or ratifying acts which are not only crim-

---

[18] Glueck, pp. 31–32. Even the most distinguished German legal scholars applied a perverted, justifying rationalization to the war crimes problem, which clearly demonstrates that the peculiar and dangerous chauvinistic "reasoning" that the world attributes to Nazi-Germany's leaders had its origin much earlier. See Professor Lauterpacht's references to the Opinion of Professor Meurer as reflecting the reasoning of German jurists on the Commission on War Crimes appointed by the German *Reichstag* after the first World War. Lauterpacht, *"The Law and the Punishment of War Crimes"* (1944) 21 *Brit. Y. B. Int. L.* 58, 61, n.1. But see Schücking, "Die deutschen Professoren und der Weltkrieg," in 5 *Flugschriften des Bundes "Neues Vaterland"* (1915).

inal according to generally accepted principles of domestic penal law but also contrary to that international law to which all States are perforce subject. Its agents, in performing such acts, are therefore acting outside their legitimate scope; and must, in consequence, be held personally liable for their wrongful conduct. It is interesting to note that a similar view on the part of the German Supreme Court may be deduced from its judgment in the case of Lieutenant-General Carl Stenger, tried in 1920 for the slaying of wounded French soldiers during the first World War:

> The lawfulness or unlawfulness of an act of war is determined by the rules of international law. The killing of enemies in war *is in accordance with the will of the State* which wages the war and *whose laws are decisive for the question of legality or illegality only to the extent that it is done under the conditions and within the limits which international law establishes.*[19]

It is perfectly obvious that the application of a universal principle of non-responsibility of a State's agents could easily render the entire body of international law a dead letter. For any group of criminally minded persons comprising the temporary Government that has seized power in a State could readily arrange to declare all of its violations of the law of nations—either in initiating an illegal war or in con-

---

[19] *Drucksachen des Reichstags,* I. Wahlperiode (1920) Aktenstück Nr. 2584, pp. 2563, 2568 (author's translation; italics supplied).

ducting it contrary to the laws and customs of recognizedly legitimate warfare—to be "acts of State." Thus all its treaty obligations and international law generally could be rendered nugatory; and thus the least law-abiding member of the Family of Nations could always have a weapon with which to emasculate the very law of nations itself. The result would be that the most lawless and unscrupulous leaders and agents of a State could never be brought to account. If such a State won an aggressive war, the politicians, militarists and industrialists who had planned, ordered or executed even the most flagrant atrocities and cynical breaches of international and municipal law, would of course not subject themselves to prosecution in their own courts. And if they happened to lose—as Germany and its chronic militarists have in our day happened twice to do—they would again be assured of personal immunity through application of an irrational technicality. Only the State would have to pay reparations; and that would mean that either the war-impoverished losing State would gradually wiggle out of its obligation, and even transform it into a loss to the people of the victor State (as was true of Germany vis à vis the United States after the first World War); or many ordinary citizens of the losing State, who had had nothing to do with initiating or conducting an unjust and ruthless war, would be penalized through heavy taxation to meet the fine imposed upon their nation. The scoundrels at the top, who had actually plotted and carried out the breaches of international and municipal law, would conveniently escape with their lives and fortunes and conserve their strength for still another try at world domination—a process in which they have nothing to lose and everything to gain.

If a doctrine so contrary to reason and justice has indeed been accepted as unconditionally valid international law, it is high time the error were remedied.[20] "It is an universal principle of jurisprudence that in cases otherwise doubtful the rule or interpretation which gives the most reasonable results [is] to be applied; and the law of nations is as much entitled to the benefit of that principle as any other kind of law."[21] Since law is supposed to embody the rule of reason in the interests of justice, and the unqualified

[20] Article 3 of the Washington treaty of February 6, 1922, dealing with the use of submarines and noxious gases in warfare (ratified by the United States of America, the British Empire, Italy and Japan) specifically provided that for determination of the guilt of the attacking *individual*, it shall be immaterial whether or not the attacker "is under orders of a governmental superior," the offender being "deemed to have violated the laws of war and . . . liable to trial and punishment as if for an act of piracy . . . before the civil or military authorities of any Power within the jurisdiction of which he may be found." France's failure to ratify rendered the treaty abortive, but her action was not based upon a lack of sympathy with the provision regarding personal liability for acts of State.

[21] Pollock, "The Sources of International Law" (1902) 2 *Col. L. Rev.* 511, 514.

act-of-State doctrine emasculates both reason and justice, it cannot be regarded as sound law.[22]

There was therefore ample justification for the disavowal of the act-of-State doctrine in both the report to the President (June 7, 1945) by the American Chief of Counsel and the Charter of the International Military Tribunal.[23] The idea that the act-of-State doctrine is universally and unconditionally operative is simply bad law; and bad law should be replaced with good law.

Where error has been detected as society has advanced, the customary law has been gently modified; it has been modified by the same power to which it owed its existence, and by which alone it can be modified—the expressed or tacit consent of nations; and by this it may still further be altered, when improvements shall be suggested by the greater progress of human society.[24]

---

[22] It is the above basis, and not the one stated in the following quotation, that justifies the prosecution of individuals for the planning and execution of an aggressive war: "One difficulty with that reply is that the body of growing custom to which reference is made is custom directed at sovereign states, not at individuals. Aside from the abortive submarine convention of 1922, where is the convention or treaty which places obligations upon the individual not to aid in waging an aggressive war?" Wyzanski, *The Nuremberg War Criminals Trial* (a communication to the American Academy of Arts and Sciences, Dec. 12, 1945) p. 3.

[23] *Trial of War Criminals*, pp. 3–4, 8, 17.

[24] Manning, *Commentaries on the Laws of Nations* (Amos ed., 1875), p. 82.

CHAPTER V

Are Individuals Liable Under International Law?

It has been objected that, even assuming aggressive war to be a crime, and assuming the invalidity of the act-of-State doctrine for the issue before the Nuremberg tribunal, the law of nations cannot be applied directly to individuals. This is true, it is argued, because in the first place international law is a body of norms applicable only to the actions of sovereign States and, in the second place, it provides no sanctions of a nature applicable to individuals, no punishments for natural persons. Thus, we are told that it is an "orthodox principle that individuals are not subjects of the law of nations"; there is an absence ". . . of international war crimes chargeable either to the collectivity of persons forming a nation or to its members individually . . . In the absence of international authority, international conventions on the conduct of warfare as a rule make it the duty of States to transform or incorporate their provisions into national regulations and to enforce the latter against the persons subject to their control." [1]

Historically, and in a practical sense, this traditional view is open to question.

To cite a familiar case, violation of the rule that prohibits piracy—regardless of whether or not that offense has also been previously constituted a crime by the statutory law of the State which happens to have seized the pirate—is clearly a violation of a norm of the law of nations. On the one hand, no prior international legislative enactment making a piratical act a crime was necessary to the criminalization or piracy; on the other hand, no prior enactment of municipal law was necessary to make the act also a local crime. Yet individuals are prosecuted as pirates.

So, also, those American States which administer the common law of crimes have from the beginning

---

[1] Manner, "The Legal Nature and Punishment of Criminal Acts of Violence Contrary to the Laws of War" (1943) 37 *Am. J. Int. L.,* pp. 407–410. A convincing series of studies in opposition to the traditional view has in recent years grown up. See Politis, *The New Aspects of International Law* (1928) and references therein; Verdross, *Die völkerrechtswidrige Kriegshandlung und der Strafanspruch der Staaten* (1920), pp. 33 *et seq.;* Schwarzenberger, "War Crimes and the Problem of an International Criminal Court" in *Czechoslovak Yearbook of International Law* (1942), pp. 67–69; Aufricht, "Personality in International Law" (1943) 37 *Am. Pol. Sci. Rev.,* pp. 217, 235–43; Kelsen, "Collective and Individual Responsibility in International Law with Particular Regard to the Punishment of War Criminals" (1943) 31 *Calif. L. Rev.,* pp. 531, 534–38. And compare *Ex parte* Quirin, 317 U.S. 1, 27–28 (1942).

punished violations of the law of nations by individuals, without prior legislative prohibition of them as crimes. Thus in Pennsylvania a defendant was convicted and sentenced to imprisonment and fine for insulting and threatening bodily harm to the Secretary of the French Legation.[2] The indictment set forth that the victim was then "under the protection of the law of nations and this Commonwealth." [3] The prosecution argued "the necessity of sustaining the law of nations . . . the connection between the law of nations and the municipal law, and the effect which the decision of this case must have upon the honor of Pennsylvania, and the safety of her citizens abroad. . . . Upon the same principle that the infringement of a statute is an indictable offense, though the mode of punishment is not pointed out in the act itself, an offense against the laws of nations, while they compose a part of the law of the land, must necessarily be indictable." [4] The court rejected the defendant's contention that "the reparation sought, and the remedy offered, are confined to the *municipal law of Pennsylvania,* where the offense was committed; and [that] in all cases of menaces, the law of Pennsylvania yields no further relief than the imposition of a legal restraint on the execution of those menaces." [5] It expressed

[2] *Respublica v. De Longchamps,* 1 Dall. 11 (Pa. 1784).

[3] *Ibid.*

[4] *Ibid.*

[5] *Id.* at 113 (italics supplied).

the opinion that the case "must be determined on the principles of the *law of nations,* which form a part of the municipal law of Pennsylvania; and, if the offenses charged in the indictment have been committed, there can be no doubt, that those laws have been violated." [6] In imposing sentence of a large fine, two years' imprisonment and the furnishing of heavy "security to keep the peace, and be of good behavior to all public Ministers, Secretaries to Embassies and Consuls . . . for seven years . . . ," the court said:

The first crime in the indictment is an infraction of the law of nations. This law, in its full extent, is part of the law of this State, and is to be collected from the practice of different nations and the authority of writers. The person of a public minister is sacred and inviolable. Whoever offers any violence to him, *not only affronts the Sovereign he represents, but also hurts the common safety and well-being of nations—he is guilty of a crime against the whole world.*[7]

The Supreme Court of the United States, in the *Saboteurs' Case,*[8] has more recently held, in effect, that individual offenders against the laws and customs of warfare can be punished under the law of warfare branch of the common law of nations, without prior

---

[6] *Id.* at 114 (italics supplied).

[7] *Id.* at 116 (italics supplied).

[8] *Ex parte* Quirin, 317 U. S. 1 (1942). And see "In the Matter of Yamashita," 14 *U. S. L. Week* 414 (Feb. 4, 1946).

intervention of specific domestic legislation. Careful examination of that decision will show it to be very probably correct to say, with Professor Hyde, that it "is impressive judicial testimony to the effect not only that" [9] the "law of nations may, and oftentimes does, address its injunctions to *individuals* by attaching an *internationally* illegal quality to particular acts," [10] but that "the law of war as a part of the law of nations is a part of the local law," [11] and "also that its applicability by the courts in reference to penal matters need not await precise legislative appraisal or definition." [12]

During the trial of German war criminals after the close of World War I, by the German Supreme Court at Leipzig, that tribunal, also, was impelled to acknowledge the direct obligatoriness of the law of nations upon individuals. In the decision of the case involving the torpedoing of the British hospital ship

---

[9] Hyde, "Aspects of the Saboteur Cases" (1943) 37 *Am. J. Int. L.* 88 (italics supplied). One of the arguments of the defense was that there is a "serious question as to whether there was any such offense as the violation of the law of war." This was probably based on the theory that inasmuch as Congress has been given specific power by the Constitution (Art. I, Sec. 8) to define offenses against the law of nations, there can be no offense of this kind in the absence of a specific statute, in accordance with the doctrine in *United States* v. *Hudson,* 7 Cranch 32 (U. S. 1812). See also "In the Matter of Yamashita," 14 *U. S. L. Week* 414 (Feb. 4, 1946).

[10] Hyde, *supra* note 9 at 91 (italics supplied).

[11] *Id.* at 88.

[12] *Id.* at 88.

Llandovery Castle and the machine-gunning of survivors in lifeboats, the German court said:

The firing on the boats was an offense against the *law of nations.* . . . *Any violation of the law of nations in warfare is* . . . *a punishable offense,* so far as in general a penalty is attached to the deed. . . . The rule of *international law,* which is here involved, is simple and is universally known. . . . The court must in this instance affirm Patzig's guilt of killing contrary to *international law.*[13]

It might be pointed out, moreover, that at the time the accused committed the offense, the Weimar Constitution, with its specific embodiment of the law of nations into the law of the German Republic, was not yet in force.

The authorities cited and others [14] amply support the conclusion that the relevant principles of the law of nations may and do obligate individuals; and that there is nothing in international law itself that necessarily prohibits the direct application of its relevant prohibitions to natural persons, if a State chooses to do so. The duty of a State as a member of the Family

---

[13] (1922) 16 *Am. J. Int. L.* 721 (italics supplied). So, also, on other occasions some of the decisions of German courts "seem to indicate a willingness on the part of some German judges, at least, to apply customary international law directly." *Masters, International Law in National Courts* (1932), p. 46.

[14] See 2 Halleck, *International Law* (4th ed. 1908), p. 351 n. 1. See also 75 *British and Foreign State Papers* (1883–84), pp. 672–75; 74 *id.* (1882–83), p. 591.

of Nations to punish violations of the prohibitions imposed by the law of nations is a matter of international law; but whether any particular local sovereignty requires prior specific "implementation" of international law by "conversion" of its prohibitions into those of municipal criminal or military law, or prefers to punish them directly without such intercession of domestic legislation, is a matter of each State's own constitution—an arrangement of municipal law. No State whose national is being proceeded against in a foreign State's criminal or military court has any right to insist that before the defendant can be prosecuted for acts obnoxious to international law the prohibitions of that system of law must first have been "transformed" into the prosecuting State's statutory criminal law. All it can claim is the same treatment of its nationals as is afforded the prosecuting State's own subjects.

Consequently, when the great majority of civilized States, after due warning to the Axis leaders, united in prosecuting individuals for violating the tenets of international law they were doing no more than could have been done had each of them proceeded individually. Indeed, they are doing a service to the Family of Nations and its international law, in combining their individual jurisdictions into a single agency speaking on behalf of world law and order. The same considerations that led to the universal recognition that pirates were violators of the law common to all

States and could therefore be prosecuted by any, apply, only with much more force, to the kind of acts committed by the Nazi leaders, especially the planning, launching, and conducting of a series of aggressive wars in violation of the most solemn treaty obligations and of international law generally. In the absence of a world authority and an international criminal tribunal, the prosecutions had perforce in the past to be conducted in the courts of the State which seized the pirate, and the punishment had to be meted out by that State; but the violation of the law involved always was one which concerned the entire Community of Nations, and the prosecuting State was acting, in effect, as agent of all civilized States in vindicating the law common to them all. However, given an international court such as the International Military Tribunal at Nuremberg, the task of trying and sentencing individuals accused of violating international law can more appropriately be performed by such a court as agent of the entire Family of Nations.

But it is also objected that international law provides no sanctions applicable to natural persons.

This claim, too, is open to question. Grotius, the father of international law, clearly implies that the law of nations provides for the death penalty in case of its violation by individuals: "There is no danger from prisoners and those who have surrendered or desired to do so; therefore in order to warrant their execution it is necessary that a crime shall have been previously committed, such a crime, moreover, as a just judge would hold punishable by death." [15]

Any lesser punishment is merely a matter of grace to the offender; and a State (or a group of States acting jointly as agent of the Family of Nations) is free under international law to impose the penalties it deems appropriate to the particular offense.[16]

Holland, a distinguished twentieth-century authority, after an exhaustive study of the most reliable sources of customary international law, also concludes that:

Individuals offending against the laws of war are liable to such punishment as is prescribed by the military code of the belligerent into whose hands they may fall, or, in default of such code, then to such punishment as may be ordered in accordance with the laws and usages of war, by a military court.[17]

---

[15] Grotius, *De Jure Belli ac Pacis*, bk. III, c. XI § 16, Cl. 1. Compare *Respublica* v. *De Longchamps*, 1 Dall. 111, 117 (Pa. 1784).

[16] Elsewhere I have gone into some of the complex political, ethical and penologic issues involved in the determination of appropriate punishment for those Nazi leaders who will be convicted. Glueck, pp. 171–77.

[17] Holland, *The Laws and Customs of War on Land as Defined by the Hague Convention of 1899* (1904), p. 45. See also Bartlett, "Liability for Official War Crimes" (1919) 35 *L. Q. Rev.*, 177, 186. "A military commission may impose any lawful and appropriate sentence, including death or life imprisonment." "Military Government" (U.S. War Dept., *Basic Field Manual*, FM 27–5, 1940), 15.

Furthermore, most States, including Germany, have long provided for various appropriate punishments of individual violators of the laws and customs of war.

These authorities speak, to be sure, of breaches of the "laws of war"; but the same principle would apply to breaches of any other prohibition of international law capable of being violated by individuals, including a breach of the peace of the world by the initiation and conduct of an illegal and criminal war.

Moreover, the situation with reference to the execution of sentence and the imposition of punishment on those of the accused at Nuremberg who will be found guilty is much more favorable than that which is usual with international courts. "The imperfect state of the law of nations, in respect that it lacks a cosmopolitan judicial court with power to execute its decrees, is a well-worn topic . . . it seems fit to be considered that in the early history of all jurisdictions the executive power at the disposal of the courts has been rudimentary, if indeed they had such power at all." [18] The International Criminal Court sitting at Nuremberg, on the other hand, has, at its disposal, the United Nations Control Council. Article 29 of the Charter, which is part of the Four-Power Agreement of August 8, 1945, to which many States have since acceded, provides that "In case of guilt, sentences shall be car-

---

[18] Pollock, *supra* p. 35, note 26, at 514.

ried out in accordance with the orders of the Control Council and the Control Council may at any time reduce or otherwise alter the sentences but may not increase the severity thereof." [19]

---

[19] Trial of War Criminals, p. 21.

CHAPTER VI

Are the Nuremberg Proceedings Illegal?

It will be seen from the foregoing that it is not doing unpardonable violence to the law to exclude both the act-of-State argument and that which insists that international law is not and cannot ever be applicable to individual offenders. However, in the statement of November 21, 1945, made by counsel for the defense at the opening of the Nuremberg trial, the claim was insistently urged that to hold the accused, as individuals, for acts of State was ex post facto and unjust. It was argued that until that trial, jurists and nations had:

. . . never even thought of incriminating statesmen, generals and economic leaders of a State using force, and still less bringing these men before an international criminal court. . . . As far as crimes against peace are concerned, the present trial has, therefore, no legal basis in international law but is a procedure based on a new penal law; a penal law created only after the act. This is in contradiction to a legal principle that is cherished in the world. It has been violated partly in Hitler Germany. This violation has been emphatically disapproved within and without the Reich. This principle is the maxim: punishment is possible only if a law has been violated that was in existence at the time the act was committed and that provided punishment. . . . This principle is not a matter of opportunism but based on the knowledge that every defendant must feel treated unjustly if he is punished under a murder law created *ex post facto*.[1]

One may perhaps be pardoned for viewing with some skepticism this sudden Wagnerian trumpet-call against the terrible legal sin of "a murder law created ex post facto." The Nazis, who through their lawyers now nobly enter the lists to slay the fire-breathing dragon of retroactive liability, were not particularly famous for their interest in such a holy crusade when they were in power and dealt with their numerous victims. Indeed, to justify most of their tortures, mass-murders and mass-lootings, the Nazis were not greatly troubled about the existence of *any* law—retroactive or other. Since the administration of justice does not operate in a vacuum it is perhaps not altogether ir-relevant, in judging the theory and proceedings of the Nuremberg trial, to advert to the fact that the defend-ants there, who evidently insist upon a strictly tech-nical interpretation of law only when such an inter-pretation will redound to their benefit, do not come into court with clean hands. Nor were many members of the German bar and bench altogether unsympa-thetic with the Nazi lawlessness. It is notorious that

[1] *New York Times*, Nov. 22, 1945, p. 3, col. 1. (The official tran-script was not available.)

a great deal of clear and serious ex-post-facto legislation was enacted or decreed in Nazi Germany.

For example: "Whoever commits an act which . . . deserves punishment according to the principles of criminal law and to the *sound feelings of the people,* [i.e., the Nazis] will be punished." [2] The Nazis also prosecuted and punished many nationals of the countries they overran, for alleged crimes committed before 1939, the acts of which, by the laws of those countries, were not crimes at that time. Although the German constitution of 1919 contained a clause prohibiting ex-post-facto laws, this did not prevent the Nazi Government from retroactively changing arson from a non-capital to a capital crime in the Van der Lubbe Reichstag fire case in 1933. So, also, following the murderous "purge" of Roehm and his companions during the falling-out of the Nazi gangsters, Hitler later "legalized" the "executions."

The claim (in the quotation) of counsel for the Nuremberg defendants that violation of the principle, *nulla poena sine lege* was *"emphatically disapproved within the Reich"* is something that will call for a great deal of proof before it is acceptable; and the indignant protest against alleged retroactive liability made by the Germans at Nuremberg may be taken with a rather large grain of salt.

[2] Section 2 of the law concerning alteration of the criminal code, June 28, 1935, *Reichsgesetzblatt* (1935) I, Art. 1, §z, p. 839 (italics supplied).

Not so the support of their position by certain American lawyers, as to whose sincerity there can be no doubt.[3]

It is therefore necessary to examine the supposed "retrospective"[4] nature and consequent injustice allegedly involved in the Nuremberg trial and particularly in holding individual members of a lawless Government criminally responsible for their deeds.

The doctrine, "no crime and no punishment without pre-existing law," has a long and honorable pedigree;[5]

---

[3] See, *e.g.*, these thought-provoking articles: Radin, "War Crimes and the Crime of War" (1945) 21 *Va. L. Q.* 497–516; Vambery, "Law and Legalism" (1945) 161 *Nation* 573; "The Nürnberg Novelty," (1945) 32 *Fortune* 140–141; Wyzanski, *The Nuremberg War Criminal Trial, op. cit.*, (hereinafter cited as, Wyzanski); Konvitz, "Will Nuremberg Serve Justice?" (1946) 1 *Commentary* (American Jewish Committee) 9–15; Hula, "Punishment for War Crimes" (1946) 13 *Social Research* 1–23.

[4] While it is true that "retrospective" or "retroactive" laws must for certain purposes be distinguished from constitutionally prohibited ex-post-facto criminal statutes [see *Calder* v. *Bull*, 3 Dall. 386 (U.S. 1798)], the terms are used interchangeably in the text, since no ambiguity can result, and Continental lawyers most frequently speak of "retroactive" or "retrospective" legislation.

[5] See authorities cited by Shulman, "Retroactive Legislation" in (1937) 13 *Encyc. Soc. Sci.*, p. 355; Smead, "The Rule Against Retroactive Legislation: A Basic Principle of Jurisprudence" (1936) 20 *Minn. L. Rev.* 775; Hall, "Nulla Poena Sine Lege" (1937) 47 *Yale L. J.* 165; Wyzanski. Some American sources for the constitutional prohibition of ex-post-facto laws (Art. I, Sec. 9, cl. 3; Sec. 10, cl. 1) are the Maryland and North Carolina Declarations of Rights of 1776, the Massachusetts Constitution of 1780, and the New Hampshire Constitution of 1784. Fisher, *The Evolution of the Constitution of the United States* (1897), pp. 210–211.

but there has been a tendency to insist upon its literal observance regardless of the factual question whether its non-application formally, in a given set of circumstances, will or will not actually work an injustice. One can understand the spirit with which, in domestic constitutional law, the application of the ex-post-facto test to legislation is jealously insisted upon. For it is rightly concluded that "the antagonism to *ex post facto* laws rests upon this sound principle: if the law can be created after the offense then power is absolute and arbitrary . . . (the very notion which is most repugnant to constitutionalism)." [6] But the essence of the doctrine in question as applied to a novel situation can only be grasped when one views its actual effects upon the person accused of crime.

The reason, the humanity, and consequently the social policy, behind the doctrine, *nulla poena sine lege* are based upon an avoidance of unfairness to the accused which, when analyzed, is shown to involve the following elements:

(1) It is unjust to punish for an act which prior to its commission was not officially prohibited, because to do so would be to change, arbitrarily, the legal consequences of an act.

---

[6] Wyzanski, p. 3. See Story, *A Familiar Exposition of the Constitution of the United States* (1883), p. 144.

(2) The failure to prohibit the act until after it was done is particularly obnoxious to justice, because, inasmuch as the prohibition of retroactive penal legislation involves the principle that all conduct *not* legally prohibited is *permissible*, the act in question is typically one which, according to prevailing popular opinion and legislative belief at the time it was done, was deemed harmless or at least relatively venial.[7]

(3) It is unjust to punish for such an act, because the prospective malefactor had received no prior notice that his deed would be punished.

(4) The law supposedly violated, notice of the existence of which had not been given, must at all events have been enacted by a sovereign to which the accused was subject, and one vested with authority and power to prohibit and punish acts deemed harmful to the general welfare.

---

[7] "There is still a more unreasonable method than this, which is called making of laws *ex post facto;* when after an action (*indifferent in itself*) is committed, the legislator then for the first time declares it to have been a crime, and inflicts a punishment upon the person who has committed it. Here it is impossible that the party could foresee that an action, *innocent when it was done*, should be afterwards converted to guilt by a subsequent law; he had therefore no cause to abstain from it; and all punishment for not abstaining must of consequence be cruel and unjust." Blackstone, 1 *Commentaries,* *46 (italics supplied). Historically, ex post facto penalization for *serious* acts has been very rare. For a few illustrations, see *King* v. *Thurston,* 1 Lev. 91, 83 Eng. Rep. 312 (1663); *Calder* v. *Bull,* 3 Dall. 386, 389 (U.S. 1798).

The analyzing of the issue and its ramifications thus tangibly, in terms of what ex post facto application of law means to the accused, ought to disclose whether or not, in *substance* if not in literal form, any real retroactivity or true injustice is involved in prosecuting the Nazi leaders as personally responsible for planning and executing aggressive wars.

(1) Is it changing the legal consequences of the aggressive acts of warfare and their instrumental mass-murders and mass-thefts to hold the Nazi leaders personally responsible? It has been argued, above, that because of the status of custom among the vast majority of peoples in our day, aggressive warfare may legitimately be regarded as an international crime. It has further been argued that it is very doubtful if the act-of-State doctrine, by which the accused seek immunity, ever was sound law so far as concerns its applicability to the kind of deeds done by the Nazi leaders. If the International Military Tribunal, representing many of the States of the Family of Nations and the great majority of civilized peoples, should decide that as a matter of reasonable law aggressive war is nowadays a crime and the act-of-State principle is not applicable to the Nazi leaders, there could be no sound reason for the claim that they were being held liable retrospectively; for the court would

then be merely settling an unsettled state of the law by a reasonable construction of the law.[8]

(2) Are the acts involved in the waging of an aggressive war such as, were it not for the supposed holding of them to be criminal only after they were committed, would generally be regarded as quite harmless? It was pointed out in the argument of counsel in the Nuremberg trial that the *nulla poena sine lege* principle is "based on the knowledge that every defendant must feel treated unjustly if he is punished under a murder law created *ex post facto.*" This very quotation gives their whole case away: for it speaks of a "*murder* law created *ex post facto.*" In other words, it is brazenly claimed that because the civilized world cannot put its finger on some specific section in

---

[8] Compare a similar argument by *Wyzanski* 2, speaking of the unsettled state of the law of "superior orders": "If the International Military Tribunal in connection with a charge of a war crime, *stricto sensu,* refuses to recognize superior orders as a defense it will not be making a retroactive determination or applying an *ex post facto* law. Proof of that assertion is this: suppose tomorrow the grand jury for the District of Massachusetts should indict Private Jones for whipping a German prisoner of war at Fort Devens, and the private defended himself on the ground that he was obeying the order of the commanding officer at Devens,—would not the District Judge face the precise problem the Nüremberg tribunal now faces? And if the District Judge should decide adversely to Jones would any reasonable person say that construction of the law was a violation of the *ex post facto* clause of the United States Constitution, Article I, s. 9?" (Incidentally, both the United States and the British Rules of Warfare greatly weakened the superior orders defense during the course of the war.)

an international penal code which prohibits the slaughter of millions in an aggressive, unlawful and unnecessary war, such acts were *permissible* since, technically, they were not labeled "murder" by world law at the time the killings occurred, even though by the laws of all civilized States unjustified killings are stigmatized as murders.[9] Even to state the German lawyers' proposition is to demonstrate its melange of impudence, cynicism, and absurdity.

(3) But in addition to the argument that those acts which are not specifically prohibited by some international penal code are permissible—however terrible and dangerous to the rest of humanity they may be, and however universally they are deemed crimes— there is the further argument that to hold men retroactively responsible is bad because the accused had no advance notice that the acts they were about to do were to be punished as crimes; otherwise, presumably, they would not have done them. Now what are the facts with respect to the defendants at Nuremberg? Can they seriously claim injured innocence because of lack of advance notice that their acts would be regarded as crimes? Surely, Hitler, Goebbels, Himmler, Goering, Frank, Doenitz, Keitel, Ribbentrop, Schacht, and the rest of those in the inner political military and economic circle of the Nazi Government knew that Germany had signed and ratified a

[9] See Appendix A.

solemn treaty which outlawed war and in which it agreed to resort only to peaceful methods of settling international disagreements.[10] Surely they knew that Germany had again and again entered into treaties with its neighbors in which it solemnly assured them of peaceful and friendly intentions.[11] Surely, also, the leading Nazis on trial at Nuremberg knew of the international pronouncements which conceived of a war of aggression as an international crime. And surely they knew that a State could not unilaterally make a mere "scrap of paper" of such basic security treaties as the Briand-Kellogg Pact [12] and Germany's numerous engagements to settle international disputes by pacific means only.

---

[10] In the German reply to the letter of the American Ambassador proposing the Treaty for the Renunciation of War (April 27, 1928), the German Government (by Stresemann) had welcomed ". . . most warmly the opening of negotiations for the conclusion of an international pact for the outlawry of war." *Treaty for the Renunciation of War* (Dept. of State Publication 468, 1933), p. 40.

[11] For details of the numerous treaties entered into and violated by Germany during her orgy of aggression, see Appendix C to Indictment Number I, "Charges and Particulars of Violations of International Treaties, Agreements and Assurances Caused by the Defendants in the Course of Planning, Preparing and Initiating the Wars," *Trial of War Criminals*, pp. 82–89.

[12] "A signatory State cannot by denunciation or nonobservance of the Pact release itself from its obligations thereunder." "Articles of Interpretation Proposed by the Committee on Conciliation Between Nations of The International Law Association," Report of the *Thirty-Eighth Conference, Budapest,* 1934 (1935) p. 4, Art. 3.

Not only did they know all this, but they had had notice from Versailles of the strong view expressed by all but the American and Japanese members of the Commission on Responsibility at the close of World War I that "all persons belonging to enemy countries, however high their position may have been, without distinction of rank, including Chiefs of States, who have been guilty of offenses against the laws and customs of war or the laws of humanity, are liable to criminal prosecution." [13] Certainly it may be said that the waging of an aggressive, unnecessary and particularly brutal war is a crime against "the laws of humanity." And, again, the Germans were warned at Versailles that, ". . . in the hierarchy of persons in authority, there is no reason why rank, however exalted, should in any circumstances protect the holder of it from responsibility when that responsibility has been established before a properly constituted tribunal." [14]

Furthermore, they had notice again and again, from Roosevelt, Churchill, and Stalin, as well as from groups of statesmen of the lesser Powers—all on behalf of the united front of law-abiding nations—that they would be held responsible personally and individually

[13] "Commission on the Responsibility of the Authors of the War and on Enforcement of Penalties" (1920) 14 *Am. J. Int. L.* 95, 117. The American and Japanese Representatives on the Commission filed Memoranda of Reservations. *Id.* at 127 and 151.

[14] *Id.* at 116.

for their crimes.[15] While some of these pronounce-ments emphasized barbarities committed against civilians, hostages, and prisoners of war, others spoke in general terms of the Nazi crimes, without specifi-cally excluding the parent crime of a war of aggression which made possible the numerous murders, rapes, thefts, and other derivative crimes; and one at least, Stalin's speech of November 6, 1943, specifically an-nounced the necessity of the Allies sternly punishing "Fascist criminals, guilty instigators of the present war. . . ." [16]

Not only has the evidence introduced at the Nurem-berg trial shown that Hitler and his clique well knew they were trampling international law under foot, but also that they deliberately planned to use and did use assurances of their adherence to international obliga-tions as political soporifics to lull the law-abiding na-

[15] The United Nations Commission for the investigation of War Crimes, established in October, 1942, after referring to the different classes of atrocities of which it would take cognizance, stated as among its functions, "to investigate, consider and report upon *any other instances or classes of war crimes* referred to them by the general consent of the Governments of the United Nations." The Declaration of St. James's Palace begins with the words: "Whereas Germany, since the beginning of the present conflict *which arose out of her policy of aggression,* has instituted in the occupied coun-tries a regime of terror characterized among other things by im-prisonments, mass expulsions, the execution of hostages and massacres," etc. *Punishment for War Crimes* (The Inter-Allied In-formation Committee, 1942) 3 (italics supplied). See also Ap-pendix B.

[16] *New York Times,* November 7, 1943, p. 45, col. 7.

tions into a false sense of security and to conceal an elaborate and ruthless program of universal lawlessness, murder, rapine, and plunder. At the same time they threatened, to a world at once amazingly gullible and hopefully unbelieving, that they would trample all law under foot. "I shall shrink from nothing," shouted Hitler. "No so-called international law, no agreements will prevent me from making use of any advantage that offers." [17] And again, "These so-called atrocities spare me a hundred thousand individual actions against disobedience and discontent." [18]

Surely, also, Hitler, Himmler, Goering, Ribbentrop, Frank, Keitel, Doenitz, and the rest of the unholy alliance in supreme authority in Nazi Germany knew full well that murder is murder, whether wholesale or retail, whether committed in pursuance of a gigantic conspiracy to disregard all treaties and to wage lawless wars or of a smaller conspiracy evolved by a group of domestic murderers.

Surely, also, the accused knew that they could be executed for their deeds without being granted the privilege of any trial at all. Can they now be heard to complain that they had no notice that they would have to stand trial under an interpretation of international law which they do not like because they deem it to involve retroactivity?

[17] Rauschning, *Hitler Speaks* (1939), p. 21.
[18] *Id.* at 90.

That which Hitler and his clique did *not* know was that while they would be given every reasonable facility for defense, they would not be permitted to escape personal liability by hiding their flagrant deeds behind the protective mantle of the convenient "State." Is their ignorance of that suddenly to transform them into innocents whose prosecution is frightfully unjust, and fatally "illegal," and obnoxiously "ex post facto" because it involves something of which they had had no prior notice?

Reviewing the historic facts, it becomes abundantly clear, then, that the Nazi leaders knew that Germany's numerous unlawful and unprovoked assaults upon her peaceable neighbors constituted wars of aggression; that wars of aggression had been outlawed by the action of the great majority of civilized States including Germany, Italy, and Japan; that several international pronouncements had declared such deeds to constitute, specifically, international crimes; and that the United Nations were in no way limiting themselves with reference to the type of acts they would regard as war crimes but, on the contrary, were not unlikely to include the planning and waging of aggressive war among the criminal acts for which individuals would be held responsible.

(4) Were the accused subject to a competent sovereign who could lawfully prohibit aggressive wars and declare them to be criminal? If the pre-existence

of a single "World State" under a written World Constitution be deemed indispensable, then it must be admitted there was no such sovereign. If, however, the solidarity of opinion of practically the entire membership of the Community of Nations and its peoples (excepting largely those nations and peoples charged with the commission of the crimes in question) may be regarded as expressing the juridical consensus of civilized States, then the sovereign power emerges as an international force; for the peoples of the world have with sufficient clarity made plain their conviction that aggressive warfare is and should be punished as a crime against international peace and order. The right of law-abiding States to punish, in the name of the entire civilized Community of Nations, acts which by their nature threaten the very existence of international law itself must be regarded as inherent, by the nature of modern technologic development; for this has twice in a quarter-century enabled a single, highly industrialized nation to come close to the enslavement of the entire world. Until that elemental right was invoked at Nuremberg, it was latent, although it had been clearly foreshadowed in the Report of the Allied Committee on Responsibilities at Versailles after defeat of the Central Powers in World War I; [19] but

---

[19] See *Report of Commission on the Responsibility of the Authors of the War and on Enforcement of Penalties* (1924) 14 *Am. J. Int. L.*, p. 95 *et seq.*; Treaty of Peace with Germany, Articles 228–230 (1919) 13 *Am. J. Int. L.* (Supp.) 151, 250.

events of our century have demonstrated the indispensability of recognizing such an international jurisdiction and have also demonstrated that its emergence into the field of action cannot depend upon complete unanimity of agreement among members of the Family of Nations, since certain States have clearly proved their preference for international violence rather than international law.

On this question of sovereignty in its relation to the growth of law two points of view are possible:

In the one, the essence of law is that it is imposed upon society by a sovereign will. In the other, the essence of law is that it develops within society of its own vitality. In the one case, law is artificial: the picture is that of an omnipotent authority standing high above society, and issuing *downwards* its behest. In the other case, law is spontaneous, growing *upwards,* independently of any dominant will. The second view does not exclude the notion of sanction or enforcement by a supreme established authority. This, in most societies, becomes necessary at some stage in the ordinary course of social growth. But authority so set up and obeyed by agreement is not the sole and indispensable source of all law. It is itself a creation of law.[20]

History is on the side of the second view. For history has afforded numerous examples of varying degrees of

---

[20] Allen, *Law in the Making* (1927), p. 2. See also Schriner, *"Holmes, Austin and the Nature of Law"* in *Justice Oliver Wendell Holmes* (1936), pp. 21–29; *"Holmes on Austin's Theory of Law,"* id. at 36.

crystallization of that power disciplined by concepts of law which lies behind "sovereignty" and "jurisdiction"; and there have heretofore been periods in history when law was enforced, to the extent that it could be, by a "sovereign" whose power was as yet incompletely developed and who had to compete with other authorities in claiming jurisdiction over subjects. For example, it was not until the reign of Henry II (1154–1189) in England that national courts were developed administering law for the entire realm in vindication of the "King's Peace" through the King's judges (cf., Constitutions of Clarendon, 1164).[21] Consider, also, the jurisdictional conflicts at various stages during the vicissitudes of the Holy Roman Empire, especially periods of decay (e.g., the fifteenth to seventeenth centuries), when the authority of the emperor was successfully challenged by that of the local princelings. As to Roman antiquity, Clark points out that

. . . as a general proposition Sovereignty is not necessarily *sole*. . . . The original constitution, or pre-constitutional condition, of Rome was probably a loose kind of federation, which might be called an aristocratic democracy. The sole Sovereignty, which undoubtedly preceded the Republic, was . . . a comparatively late development, compounded of earlier offices which did not amount to Sovereignty proper. . . . Sole Sovereignty . . . even when attained, has not been historically by any means a

---

[21] 4 Blackstone, *Commentaries*, *422.

permanent institution but has sometimes had to give way to the plural, but minor, authorities which preceded it, revived under slightly different forms; sometimes, though nominally retained, [it] had to share its powers with other officials in such a manner as to reduce it to a government nominally "limited" but constituting in fact a "Corporate" Sovereignty. The history of Rome, after the fall of the Tarquinian dynasty, is, I believe, an example of the first case. On the other hand, in the Teutonic settlers in Britain, as in some Continental associations of the same and kindred stocks, an originally sole military leadership has been developed into something more nearly resembling true Sovereignty.[22]

It may be pointed out, finally, that if the founding fathers had implemented the Articles of Confederation with a court, serious conflicts of sovereignty and jurisdiction between the Confederation and the separate sovereign States might therein have been aired. For though the new Congress was given only weak powers, the Confederation would have had to try, sooner or later, to enforce such powers.[23]

---

[22] Clark, *History of Roman Private Law, Part III, Regal Period* (1919), pp. 398, 401, 386–87. See also *id.* at 455; Allen, *op. cit., supra* note 20 at pp. 5, 28 *et seq.*

[23] "The Congress itself, under the Articles of Confederation, had, within two months before the sitting of the Federal Convention, adopted resolutions, drafted by John Jay, in which it was declared that when a treaty was made and ratified by authority of those Articles, it became 'part of the law of the land, and not only independent of the will and power of the [State] Legislatures, but also binding and obligatory on them'; that all existing State laws repugnant to the treaty ought to be forthwith repealed 'to avoid the

Summarizing the historic evidence, an authority correctly concludes: "In early forms of society the conduct of men in forming legal relationships is governed by customary rules. These are recognized and followed as *law independently of any 'sovereign' injunction or enforcement.*"[24] Internationally organized society is still in such "early form" today. In acting jointly and as agent of all civilized States in the vindication of international law through the prosecution

---

disagreeable necessity there might otherwise be of raising and discussing questions touching their validity and obligation'; and further that the States ought to provide that their Courts should decide all cases according to the intent of the treaty 'anything in the Acts . . . to the contrary notwithstanding.' These resolutions were not explicit in their recognition of the right of the State Courts to disregard State statutes without express authority from the States; but they contained a clear intimation that the Congress expected that the State Courts would take such action; and it is to be noted that arguments in behalf of such action were at once made in cases in such Courts. . . . "Secret Journals of Congress," *Foreign Affairs,* March 21, 1787; see also letters of Congress to the States, April 13, 1787. While the Federal Convention was still sitting, a case was argued in the Supreme Court of Pennsylvania at the September term of 1787, *Doane's Adm'rs. v. Penhallow,* 1 Dallas 218, in which counsel argued that a law enacted by the Continental Congress, prior to the Articles of Confederation was without authority, and that actions taken under such law were null and void. The President of the Court stated that the point involved in it, 'the sovereignty of the separate States on the one hand and the supreme power of the United States in Congress assembled on the other, . . . is indeed, a momentous question'; but the case was decided on another point; see also *Respublica* v. *Gordon* (1788), 1 Dallas 233." Warren, *Congress, the Constitution, and the Supreme Court* (1925), pp. 48–49.

[24] Allen, *op. cit., supra* note 20, at p. 102. (Italics supplied.)

of individuals who brought about its wholesale violation, the United Nations needed no pre-existent World State or World Legislature to justify the jurisdiction. The agreement of the allied States, during both World Wars I and II, to pool their rights and duties in enforcement of international law as agent for the entire Family of Nations was in itself an exercise of world sovereignty in behalf of world law. Any formal charter of united action could only have been declaratory of an existent situation.

CHAPTER VII

Some Concluding Observations

The foregoing discussion justifies the conclusion, it is believed, that the waging of an aggressive war is not only unlawful but also criminal, and that there is nothing fundamentally "retrospective" or unjust either in recognizing this fact or in holding individual members of a Government personally liable for criminal acts committed in the name of the State. At the very worst, there is only formal retroactivity. If the Court at Nuremberg will decide it has jurisdiction to examine into the alleged ex post facto nature of the Count charging individual Nazi leaders with the crime of aggressive war (something that may be doubtful in view of the fact that the organic Charter of the Court, its constitution, includes the crime in question among crimes "coming within the jurisdiction of the Tribunal for which there shall be individual responsibility"), it could legitimately be argued that not even *formal* retroactivity is involved. It was shown above that the rule of universal nonliability of members of a Government invested with absolute powers, for plotting and executing wholesale violations of both international law and the principles of criminal law common to all civilized peoples, is so contrary to reason and justice and so dangerous to the security of law-abiding peoples and to the very existence of law itself, that it must be regarded as extremely doubtful whether it ever was true law. If, now, the Nuremberg Tribunal should find it to have been bad law, not even a formal retrospective liability would be involved; for the Court, after hearing argument, would declare that the law was in fact not what the accused had assumed it to be; and a defendant's mistake as to the true status of the law, even though that mistake be inevitable, cannot, under a familiar principle of penal law, be the basis of justification or excuse.[1]

The term "ex post facto" is not a legal shibboleth; it ought not to be applied blindly and mechanically, but with reason and discretion, in the light both of its historic significance and of the realities of the modern situation.

As has been shown, the progress of international custom has given recognition to and has supplied ample evidence of the fact that a war of aggression is not only a lawless war but a criminal one. But to limit liability and punishability to guilty States is to emasculate this tremendously important principle of international law. It is not the punishment of the corporate

---

[1] Kenny, *Outlines of Criminal Law* (1907), p. 62, and authorities therein cited.

entities called States that has done or will do any good in the way of deterrence. It is rather the prosecution and castigation of power-drunk heads of State and members of Governments, that give promise of whatever deterrence there may be in condign punishment. As was said in 1918 by Lord Birkenhead, then Attorney General of England, with reference to the former German Kaiser:

It is necessary for all time to teach the lesson that failure is not the only risk which a man possessing at the moment in any country despotic powers and taking the awful decision between Peace and War, has to fear. If ever again that decision should be suspended in nicely balanced equipoise, at the disposition of an individual, let the ruler who decides upon war know that he is gambling, amongst other hazards, with his own personal safety.[2]

This view was echoed by England's redoubtable war leader, Winston Churchill, on September 8, 1942, when he assured the House of Commons that

those who are guilty of Nazi crimes will have to stand up before tribunals in every land where their atrocities have been committed, in order that an indelible warning may be given to future ages and that successive generations of men may say, "So perish all who do the like again." [3]

It is true that the agencies sitting in judgment upon the acts of the Nuremberg defendants are those

---

[2] Lloyd George, *Memoirs of the Peace Conference* (1939), p. 60; see also *id.* at 63–64.

[3] *New York Times*, September 9, 1942, p. 4, col. 8.

set up by former enemies of Germany. But although it would have been preferable to establish a truly international tribunal—one containing representatives of the former Axis nations and neutrals as well as of the United Nations [4]—it by no means follows that painstakingly fair and careful administration of justice is otherwise not possible. The actions of the International Military Tribunal at Nuremberg so far have demonstrated the earnest desire of the judges to do justice fairly and according to generally accepted standards —something acknowledged by defense counsel themselves.

Surely, it will not be seriously contended that the trial of the Nazi and Japanese war criminals should have been postponed until such time as the successor governments to the Axis misrulers had clearly demonstrated to the world their sincere desire and capacity to administer justice according to civilized standards, so that they might participate in the membership of the International Criminal Court. By the time that situation could be reached, the evidence would be "cold," most of the accused and witnesses would be dead, the public would have lost all interest, the pun-

---

[4] See *Glueck*, pp. 114, 180. It should be pointed out that if an American subject were in the toils for a crime allegedly committed against German law, he would not be heard to complain in a German court that no judge of his own nationality sat on the tribunal trying him, or that German law, which he had had no hand in framing, did not apply to him.

ishments all deterrent value. Justice would thereby be completely outwitted. Nor could the few neutrals of the recent war have been entrusted with the difficult and dangerous task of prosecuting the Nazi war leaders. For example, it is extremely questionable whether Fascist Spain could have been relied upon to undertake such an enterprise and to carry it out impartially; and small Switzerland, in the shadow of a Germany that would some day again develop into a military colossus, might well have shied away from the task.

It was practical necessity, then, and not some deep-dyed plot, that compelled a prosecution before a court in which the country of the accused is unrepresented except by counsel of the defendants' own choosing and by a panel of fair-minded, legally-trained judges.

Here, again, therefore, in examining the proceedings at Nuremberg, it is the law in action rather than the law in books that should be scrutinized. It is not amiss to recall, in this connection, the Allies' reply to the same argument of "one-sided justice" raised in 1919 when it was proposed to try the former German Emperor in a special Allied tribunal:

As regards the German contention that a trial of the accused by tribunals appointed by the Allied and Associated Powers would be a one-sided and inequitable proceeding, the Allied and Associated Powers consider that it is impossible to entrust the trial of those directly responsible for offenses against humanity and international right to their accomplices in their crimes. Almost the whole world has banded itself together in order to bring to naught the German plan of conquest and dominion. The tribunals they will establish will therefore represent the deliberate judgment of the greater part of the civilized world. The Allied and Associated Powers are prepared to stand by the verdict of history as to the impartiality and justice with which the accused will be tried.[5]

Lord Digby's famous statement regarding the Strafford Bill of Attainder has been cited [6] as a warning against the United Nations' policy of subjecting the Nazi leaders to trial instead of disposing of them by summary execution as a frankly political act:

. . . There is in Parliament a double Power of Life and Death by Bill, a Judicial Power, and a Legislative; the measure of the one, is what's legally just; of the other, what is Prudentially and Politickly fit for the good and preservation of the whole. But these two, under favour, are not to be confounded in Judgment: We must not piece up want

---

[5] "Notes of a meeting held at President Wilson's House, Paris, June 13, 1919," in 16 Miller, *My Diary at the Conference of Paris* (1924), pp. 400–1. *Cf.*, Jackson, *The Case Against the Nazi War Criminals* (1946), p. 71: "The agreement which sets up the standards by which these prisoners are to be judged does not express the views of the signatory nations alone. Other nations with diverse but highly respected systems of jurisprudence also have signified adherence to it . . . You judge, therefore, under an organic act which represents the wisdom, the sense of justice, and the will of nineteen governments, representing an overwhelming majority of all civilized people."

[6] Wyzanski, p. 4.

of legality with matter of convenience, not the defailance of prudential fitness with a pretence of legal Justice.[7]

But examination of the policy being carried out at Nuremberg will show that the caveat in the quotation is not altogether relevant. At Nuremberg it is not "defailance of prudential fitness" that is being pieced out "with a pretence of Legal Justice." There was ample prudential and political fitness, and precedent, for the execution or imprisonment of the defendants at Nuremberg (with, possibly, one or two exceptions), without any trial at all; and the proceedings at Nuremberg are not a mere "pretense of Legal Justice." At Nuremberg prudential fitness is being implemented by the reality of legal justice. The provision of an opportunity to be heard, of counsel for the defense, of witnesses for the defense, of translations of all proof into German, of an impartial, judicially-trained tribunal is not a matter of hypocrisy, but a genuine desire to provide those accused of crime with an opportunity for explanation, justification, or excuse. To test the matter, one should lay aside the books and ask the defendants at Nuremberg whether they would have preferred summary execution or imprisonment, without formal proof of their guilt, without any chance to prepare and present a defense, without any chance to

---

[7] Quoted by McIlwain, *High Court of Parliament* (1910), p. 153, from Rushworth, *The Tryal of Thomas Earl of Strafford* (1700), p. 53.

cross-examine the witnesses for the prosecution, and without careful and fair judicial oversight of the proceedings.

But it has been objected that if wars of aggression are to be deemed international crimes, then some of the United Nations who are acting as prosecutors, especially Russia in respect to the alleged aggressive attacks on Poland and Finland, ought to be willing to subject their actions to the scrutiny of the International Criminal Court.[8] Without knowing the inside facts more thoroughly than have thus far been disclosed, it is impossible to pass judgment.[9] The case of Germany's wholesale aggressions is in the meantime crystal clear. Unquestionably, where "probable cause" exists that a State has conducted a war of aggression, that State ought, ideally, to be haled before the International Tribunal. But it should be pointed out that in the meantime the question whether Russia is or is not guilty of a war of aggression is not relevant to the present issue before the court at Nuremberg. There the question is whether or not Germany and her agents

---

[8] Wyzanski, p. 8: "And what is most serious is that there is doubt as to the sincerity of our belief that all wars of aggression are crimes. A question may be raised whether the United Nations are prepared to submit to scrutiny the attack of Russia on Poland, or on Finland, or the American encouragement to the Russians to break their treaty with Japan, or the American transfer to England of 50 destroyers in what to many seems a disregard of the principles of the *Alabama* case."

[9] See Appendix E.

are guilty of such a war. The fact that a Government—whether a domestic or an international one—is not at some particular time in a position of power and authority sufficient to prosecute all individuals whom it suspects of violating the law is no reason why it should not proceed with the prosecution of those who are within its power. If the law has indeed been violated by a party temporarily outside the power of the sovereign authority, the offense still remains; there is no statute of limitations involved. In the meantime, it cannot reasonably be argued that the prosecution of so patent and chronic an aggressor nation as Germany should be indefinitely postponed until such time as all alleged malefactors can be haled before an international court. Indeed, the solemn legal recognition at Nuremberg of the existence of such a crime as a war of aggression will be an important precedent for trying other offenders.

The fear has been expressed that the Nuremberg case might become a precedent in domestic law.[10] But the likelihood of that is extremely remote. The flow of precedent has been in the opposite direction: from the developed legal systems of municipal law to the less developed system of international law. The Nuremberg trial *will* become a precedent in interna-

---

[10] See Wyzanski, p. 4, urging that the accused should have been disposed of, as were Napoleon and the Boxer rebels, by executive or political, rather than judicial ("quasi-judicial"), action.

tional law. And what kind of precedent? One which establishes that members of Governments, military cliques, industrialists, or others actually in power in a State, who deliberately lead their country into an unjustified, inexcusable, aggressive, and therefore criminal war, may be held personally liable; and that, instead of their being disposed of politically and arbitrarily, with little or no chance to be heard in defense, the accused will be afforded every reasonable opportunity to present their case before as neutral a tribunal as the progress of world organization and world law will permit. It is difficult to see in such a precedent anything but a gain for international law, for the cause of justice, and for the goal of world security, when the alternative action of one-sided, summary execution is contemplated. Most administration of justice, in the early stages, contained some element of arbitrariness. The Nuremberg trial is being conducted under a system of law that is still in an early stage of evolution. The proceedings in Germany can most fairly be judged, not by the fact that at the present stage of world jurisdiction perfect justice cannot be had, but rather by the degree of fairness actually shown by the court. Thus far it has demonstrably acted in harmony with the highest traditions of judicial dignity and impartiality.

Finally, it may be asked, since there is less doubt about the culpability of the Nazi leaders so far as violations of the familiar laws and customs of war are concerned than there is about whether they can be convicted of the crime of launching and conducting an aggressive war, why complicate the issues before the Nuremberg court by including the latter in the bill of indictment? That is a question of policy beyond my ken. But it should be pointed out that the reason for prosecuting the Nazi leaders for the crime of aggressive war is not merely or chiefly the fact that if the launching of such a war is found to be criminal then *all* acts in pursuance of such a master-crime are criminal—whether they be within or without the laws and customs of warfare, whether they be classifiable as ordinary soldierly deeds or atrocities. That is important, but not too important; for there was ample proof to bring against the Nuremberg defendants on the ordinary counts in the indictment, without resort to the aggressive-war-is-a-crime formula. They could have been (and, judging solely from the case presented by the prosecution, they have been) shown to have violated, wholesale, practically every prohibition of either customary or conventional international law dealing with the conduct of war.

The value of establishing aggressive war as a crime and the Nuremberg defendants as master criminals in the planning, launching, and conducting of such a war is rather a moral one. If the law behind Count Two in the historic indictment is finally accepted by the Nuremberg tribunal,[11] and if, after the defense has been given ample opportunity to be heard, the charge is proved down to the hilt, the Nazi leaders will be shown to all the world, and inscribed in the book of history, in their true light: as not merely ordinary criminals, whose crimes differ from others only because there are more of them, but as national leaders who, for the first time in history, have been tried, convicted, and punished for having brought upon the world the scourge of illicit war and having thereby attacked all law and all humanity. Perhaps this is what Professor Lauterpacht had in mind when he wrote:

The law of any international society worthy of that name must reject with reprobation the view that between nations there can be no aggression calling for punishment, and it must consider the responsibility for the premeditated violation of the General Treaty for the Renunciation of War as lying within the sphere of criminal law.[12]

It would be a social value of supreme significance if, out of the courthouse at Nuremberg, the dreams of the designers of the Covenant of the League of Nations, the Geneva Protocol, the Briand-Kellogg Pact, and the Charter of the United Nations sprang to life in the form of deterrent sanctions for the assassins of world peace. It would be a heartening demonstration

[11] See p. 91.
[12] *Memorandum to Cambridge Committee on War Crimes*, 1942 (unpublished).

of a long overdue international firmness of purpose to maintain the people's peace through living law, if once and for all there were cast into the teeth of war-worshipers and war-mongers the cynical words of Field-Marshal-General Count von Moltke: "Perpetual peace is a dream, and it is not even a beautiful dream." [13]

---

[13] Holland, *Letters to "The Times" Upon War and Neutrality* (1881–1909) (1914) 25. Some of the rest of this famous letter of von Moltke's is: "War is an element in the order of the world ordained by God. In it the noblest virtues of mankind are developed . . . Without war the world would stagnate, and lose itself in materialism . . . Every law presupposes an authority to superintend and direct its execution, and international conventions are supported by no such authority. What neutral States would ever take up arms for the sole reason that, two Powers being at war, the 'laws of war' had been violated by one or both of the belligerents? For offenses of that sort there is no earthly judge." *Id.* at 25. See also the persuasive reply by Professor Bluntschli, *id.* at 27–29.

APPENDIX A

The Briand-Kellogg Pact and the Defense of "Justification"

Even if it be granted that violations of the Briand-Kellogg Pact and other international agreements do not in themselves constitute crimes—only acts of illegality—there is another valid basis for employing the Pact of Paris in connection with the prosecution of the Nazi leaders. Since the initiation and conduct of such a war of aggression is at least unlawful, all acts of warfare in pursuance thereof—whether they violate the laws and customs of war or do not do so—are illegal. They also become *criminal* in considering the effect of illegality upon the defense of "justification" in criminal law. Although a soldier, in killing an enemy soldier, is for obvious reasons usually exempt from responsibility for murder,[1] this rule of exemption nevertheless requires that the killing, even if done in warfare, be lawful. Soldiers, like civilians, are bound to act within the confines of the prevailing law. As in the case of any other type of justification which cancels liability for acts other-

---

[1] See *State* v. *Gut*, 13 Minn. 341, 357 (1868); 1 Hale, *Pleas of the Crown* (1st Am. ed. 1847) 59, 433; *Commonwealth v. Holland*, 62 Ky. 182, 183 (1864): "The act being belligerent in the legal import of that comprehensive term, it was not robbery in the technical sense"; Bishop, *Criminal Law* (9th ed. 1923) § 131, p. 86; 2 *id.* at § 631, pp. 477–8.

wise criminal (e.g., execution of a felon by the proper officer, in the prescribed manner, under a valid warrant, following lawful conviction and sentence for a capital crime), the indispensable prerequisites for exemption from liability must exist. And where an act normally prohibited (e.g., killing) is committed by a soldier, even in the course of warfare, an indispensable condition for its justification is the lawfulness of the act of warfare involved. Were *all* acts of warfare lawful, mere proof that a killing was done by a soldier would be enough to exempt him from liability; but if, for example, the killing occurred after the victim, a surrendered enemy soldier, had laid down his arms, or after an armistice had been declared and the accused had been given notice thereof, the killing would be unlawful and therefore unjustifiable.

Now lawfulness, as was correctly held by the German Supreme Court in the Leipzig trials,[2] requires the acts of the soldier to be legitimate not only under domestic criminal law, but also under the law of nations, which all States and their subjects are bound to obey. Stripped of the mantle of such legality, the act in question stands out starkly as an unjustifiable and inexcusable killing of a human being—something which, by all civilized military and civil penal codes, constitutes plain murder. Herein lies the true significance of Mr. Stimson's interpretation of the effect of the Briand-Kellogg Treaty, quoted above.[3] Aggressive war having been rendered illegal, Mr. Stimson said, "it is no

---

[2] "The Court must in this instance affirm Patzig's guilt of killing contrary to *international* law." "Judgment in case of Lieutenants Dithmar and Boldt" (1922) 16 *Am. J. Int. L.* 674, 721 (italics supplied).

[3] P. 20.

longer to be the principle around which the duties, the conduct, and the rights of nations revolve." As applied to acts chargeable as crimes, aggressive war can therefore no longer be a legal justification and shield.

It is, moreover, possible to proceed from this to the *internationalization* of domestic criminal law. The universal condemnation and the legal constituents of murder, rape, and theft in all civilized penal codes may legitimately be received by an international tribunal (in the words of Article 38 of the Statute of the Permanent Court of International Justice [4]) to demonstrate both "international custom, as evidence of a general practice accepted as law," and one of "the general principles of law recognized by civilized nations."

Such a procedure would involve no retroactivity: for if it were decided that the law to be applied by the international tribunal were the pre-existent penal law of the country in which the particular crime had been committed, there could not be the slightest argument that the procedure was ex post facto. And since the various injured States all provide in their common law and codes for the punishment of murders, rapes, and thefts, the States' decision to combine their forces in an international criminal court for the purposes of such a prosecution could also not be objected to as involving substantive retroactivity. For the definitions of such crimes, the defenses of justification

---

[4] *Publications of the Permanent Court of International Justice, Series D. No. 1* (*3rd ed.*); *The Permanent Court of International Justice, Statute and Rules* (1922) 58. For an instructive account of the application of this Article by the Permanent Court, see Pfankuchen, *Article 38 of the Statute of the Permanent Court of International Justice and International Law* (unpublished thesis in the Harvard Law School Library, 1931).

or excuse, and even the punishments are all founded on essentially the same *common denominator* of legal and moral principle. And, since the accused, if the specific acts with which they were charged were established beyond a reasonable doubt, would unquestionably be guilty of the crimes in question under domestic penal law, no practical injury of the kind involved in true ex post facto legislation would be done them in proceeding, by the method suggested, under *international* law deriving from domestic law through the channel of customary usage.

APPENDIX B

Official Pronouncements on the Treatment of War Criminals

The official pronouncements by Allied statesmen during the conduct of the war with reference to the treatment of Axis war criminals were numerous; and often promised *judicial,* rather than political, disposition:

(1) On October 25, 1941, Roosevelt and Churchill made simultaneous statements in respect to the acts of barbarity committed by the Germans. Roosevelt said: "Frightfulness can never bring peace to Europe. It only sows the seeds of hatred which will one day bring fearful retribution." (1941) 5 *U. S. Dept. of State Bull.* 317. Churchill declared: "Retribution for these crimes must henceforward take its place among the major purposes of the war." The Molotov Note of November 27, 1941 (and one of January 6, 1942), warned that the German crimes were being noted and registered, and would be punished.

(2) At an historic conference in London, the nine European Governments directly participating (the major Powers and certain others of the United Nations sent observers) adopted the Declaration of St. James's Palace on January 13, 1942, of which the following clauses are relevant: "Whereas Germany, since the beginning of the present

conflict which arose out of her policy of aggression, has instituted in the occupied countries a regime of terror characterised in particular by imprisonments, mass expulsions, the execution of hostages and massacres," etc., "The undersigned Representatives of: the Government of Belgium, the Government of Czechoslovakia, the Free French National Committee, the Government of Greece, the Government of Luxembourg, the Government of the Netherlands, the Government of Norway, the Government of Poland and the Government of Yugoslavia: (1) affirm that acts of violence thus perpetrated against the civilian populations are at variance with accepted ideas concerning acts of war and political offences, as these are understood by civilised nations, (2) take note of the declaration made in this respect on 25th October, 1941, by the President of the United States of America and by the British Prime Minister, (3) place among their principal war aims the punishment, through the channel of *organised justice*, of those *guilty* and responsible for these *crimes*, whether they have ordered them, perpetrated them or in any way participated in them, (4) determine in a spirit of international solidarity to see to it that (a) those guilty and responsible, whatever their nationality, are sought for, handed over to justice and *judged*, (b) that the *sentences* pronounced are carried out." The principles of the Declaration were accepted (January 9, 1942) by the Chinese Government, and subscribed to also (October 14, 1942) by the Government of Soviet Russia.

(3) On August 21, 1942, Roosevelt referred to the Declaration of St. James's Palace, and in condemning the crimes committed against the civil population in occupied lands, solemnly announced that "the time will come

when" the criminals "will have to stand in *courts of law* in the very countries which they are now oppressing, and to answer for their acts." (1942) 7 *U. S. Dept. of State Bull.* 709, 710.

(4) On September 8, 1942, Mr. Churchill promised that "those who are *guilty* of Nazi *crimes* will have to stand up before *tribunals* in every land where the atrocities have been committed, in order that an indelible warning may be given to future ages and that successive generations of men may say 'So perish all who do the like again.' " *New York Times,* September 9, 1942, p. 4, col. 8.

(5) On October 7, 1942, a decision was made public by Washington and London to establish a United Nations' Commission for the Investigation of War Crimes, and that named *criminals* wanted for war crimes should be arrested and handed over at the time of the armistice and as one of the conditions in the armistice, with surrender of others deemed implicated after investigation.

(6) On July 30, 1943, Roosevelt addressed a note of warning to neutral countries: ". . . There are now rumors that Mussolini and members of his Fascist gang may attempt to take refuge in neutral territory. One day Hitler and his gang and Tojo and his gang will be trying to escape from their countries. I find it difficult to believe that any neutral country would give asylum to or extend protection to any of them. I can only say that the Government of the United States would regard the action by a neutral government in affording asylum to Axis leaders or their tools as inconsistent with the principles for which the United Nations are fighting and that the United States Government hopes that no neutral government will permit its territory to be used as a place of refuge or otherwise assist such

persons in any effort to escape their just deserts." (1943) 9 *U.S. Dept. of State Bull.* 62.

(7) On April 12, 1943, a warning was sent the Japanese Government that for the barbarous executions of American aviators, "the American Government will visit upon the officers of the Japanese Government responsible for such uncivilized and inhumane acts the punishment they deserve." (1943) 8 *U.S. Dept. of State Bull.* 337, 339. A further warning was given through an official press release, January 31, 1944. (1944) 10 *U.S. Dept. of State Bull.* 145–46.

(8) A concurrent resolution regarding Nazi atrocities declared in 1943 "that it is the sense of this Congress that those guilty, directly or indirectly, of these *criminal* acts, shall be held accountable and punished in a manner commensurate with the offenses for which they are responsible." *Concurrent Res.* March 18, 1943 (57 Stat. 721, 722).

(9) The Moscow Declaration (Nov. 1, 1943) warned that "at the time of the granting of any armistice to any government which may be set up in Germany, those German officers and men and members of the Nazi party who have been responsible for, or have taken a consenting part [in the] atrocities, massacres and executions, will be sent back to the countries in which their abominable deeds were done in order that they may be *judged and punished according to the laws* of these liberated countries and of the free governments which will be erected therein," and that the "Allied Powers will pursue them to the uttermost ends of the earth and will deliver them to the accusers in order that justice may be done." (1943) 9 *U.S. Dept. of State Bull.* 310–11.

(10) In reply to a question in the House of Commons, Churchill said (September 26, 1944): "The governments

are resolved to do their utmost to prevent Nazi criminals finding a refuge in neutral territory from the consequences of their crimes. . . . It is not our intention to allow the escape of these men to be effected without exerting almost every resource which a civilized power can contemplate."

(11) The American-British-Russian Declaration of Potsdam, published July 26, 1945, announced (par. 10): ". . . stern *justice* shall be meted out to all war *criminals,* including those who have visited cruelties upon our prisoners." (1945) 13 *U. S. Dept. of State Bull.* 137–38. Arts. III. A 5 and VII of the Report on the Tripartite Conference in Berlin (Potsdam) also provides for the arrest and *bringing to judgment of war criminals,* and affirmed the intention of the three major Governments to bring "those major war *criminals* whose *crimes* under the Moscow Declaration of October 1943 have no particular geographic location . . . to swift and sure justice." (1945) 13 *U. S. Dept of State Bull.* 155, 158. By the instruments of unconditional surrender, Germany and Japan accepted the terms. (1945) 13 *U. S. Dept. of State Bull.* 105 *et seq.; Id.* at 205; *id.* at 362 *et seq.*

APPENDIX C

The Schooner Exchange v. *McFaddon and Others*

(7 Cranch 116)

The ship in question, a public armed vessel of France, commissioned by and in the service of Napoleon, came into Philadelphia after rough weather, to make necessary repairs and lay in supplies. She conducted herself in accordance with both municipal and international law. The United States was then at peace with France. As the schooner was about to depart, she was seized on process issued under a libel filed in a U. S. District Court, which alleged that her libellants had been the sole owners when, previously, she had sailed from Baltimore bound for a Spanish port; that while en route she had been seized by persons acting under decrees of the French Emperor and disposed of in violation of the libellant's rights; that a sentence of condemnation had never been pronounced against her by a court of competent jurisdiction; and that she was still the property of libellants. The United States Attorney informed the court that the schooner was a public armed vessel of a friendly power; told of the circumstances under which she had involuntarily had to enter the port of Philadelphia; pointed out that if she had been the property of libellants such property was divested and became vested in Napoleon within a port of his Empire or a country occupied by his arms, outside the jurisdiction of the United States, under the laws of France; and therefore moved dismissal of proceedings and release of the vessel. The District Court sustained the motion; the Circuit Court reversed; the Supreme Court reversed the judgment of the Circuit Court and held that the libel must be dismissed and the schooner released.

APPENDIX D

People v. *McLeod*

(25 Wend. 481 [N. Y. 1841]; 26 Wend. 663 [N. Y. 1841])

The case arose early in American history and brought about a great deal of discussion among statesmen and jurisconsults. During an insurrection in Canada in 1837 against the British Government, members of the colonial authorities' military force invaded the American steamer *Caroline* while she was moored on the American side of the Niagara River, attacked passengers believed to be insurgents, burned the steamer and set her adrift over Niagara Falls. An American citizen was killed. In 1840 McLeod, a British subject, was arrested by the New York authorities and held for trial in a state court on arson and murder charges in connection with the attack on the *Caroline*. The British minister at Washington demanded McLeod's immediate release on the ground that the destruction of the *Caroline* was a "public act of persons in Her Majesty's service, obeying the order of their superior authorities"; that therefore it could "only be the subject of discussion between the two national Governments," and could "not justly be made the ground of legal proceedings in the United States against the persons concerned."

Secretary of State Webster, while declaring that the Federal Government was then unable to comply with the demand, acknowledged the validity of the British argument: "That an individual, forming part of a public force, and acting under the authority of his Government, is not to be held answerable as a private trespasser or malefactor, is a principle of public law sanctioned by the usages of all civilized nations, and which the Government of the United States has no inclination to dispute." The New York Court refused to release McLeod at the intervention of the Federal Government, and he was tried but acquitted on proof of an alibi. The episode was followed by enactment by Congress in 1842 (5 Stat. 538, c. 257, § 1) of the provision authorizing courts of the United States to issue a writ of *habeas corpus* where a subject of a foreign State is in custody for an act done or omitted under an alleged right or privilege claimed under the sanction of a foreign State, "the validity and effect whereof depend upon the law of nations." *Cf. Underhill* v. *Hernandez,* 65 Fed. 577 (C. C. A. 2d, 1895).

Calhoun, in the Senate, contraverted the position of the British "that where a government authorizes or approves of the act of an individual, it makes it the act of the government, and thereby exempts the individual from all responsibility to the injured country." He argued that "the laws of nations are but the laws of morals, as applicable to individuals, so far modified, and no further, as reason may make necessary in their application to nations. Now, there can be no doubt that the analogous rule, when applied to individuals, is, that both principal and agents, or . . . instruments, are responsible in criminal cases; directly the reverse of the rule on which the demand for the release of McLeod is made. . . . Suppose, then, that the British, or any other government, in contemplation of war, should send out emissaries to blow up the fortifications erected, at such vast expense, for the defense of our great commercial marts . . . would the production of the most authentic papers, signed by all the authorities of the British Government, make it a public transaction, and exempt the villains from all responsibility to our laws and tribunals?" 2 Moore, *A Digest of International Law* (1906), pp. 23–30, 409–14.

It will be noted that the above transaction involved the action of a Government on *neutral* territory in *peacetime;* and the British and Webster's views of the act-of-State exemption are at all events therefore not applicable to the relations of belligerents in wartime.

Alleged Acts of Aggression on the Part of Russia and the United States

Without attempting to go into any technical definition of "aggression,"[1]—something that greatly troubled the experts on the various committees of the League of Nations,—it would seem not to be giving proper weight to differences in kind as well as degree, to place the numerous carefully planned and brutal invasions of neighboring lands by Germany on the same plane with the acts of the United States or even those of Soviet Russia, as is done in the statement in note 8, on page 98.

The "inside facts" about the Russian actions are not completely available, although some respectable proof has already been introduced at the Nuremberg trial that Finnish Government leaders were implicated in German plans of aggression against Russia. (See *New York Times*, February 9, 1946, p. 7, col. 4; *id.*, Feb. 13, 1946, p. 15, col. 4).

Japan, as an active member of the Axis, and obviously imbued with the Axis policy of ruthless conquest, was in fact an enemy of Russia as well as of the other Member-States of The United Nations, albeit technically at peace with Russia.

So far as the "destroyer deal" is concerned, the argument of Attorney General Robert H. Jackson in favor of the

[1] See Foreword by Mr. Justice Jackson.

transfer, was based on Oppenheim's international law distinction between the building of *ships to the order of a belligerent* with intent or reasonable cause to believe they would enter the service of a belligerent, and the selling of existing armed vessels to a belligerent as contraband. 39 *Ops. Att'y Gen.* (1941), 494–96 (italics supplied). (And see Briggs, "Neglected Aspects of the Destroyer Deal," 1940, 34 *Am. J. Int. L.* 569). But apart from such a technical argument, the act of the British during the American Civil War in permitting the outfitting of the *Alabama* for use of the Confederacy (*The Alabama Claims,* United States-Great Britain, Claims Arbitration, 4 *Papers Relating to the Treaty of Washington,* 1872, 49), is hardly comparable to the action of the United States in 1940, in exchanging destroyers for air bases. Before the destroyer deal was entered into, Hitler had ruthlessly trampled upon all rights of neutrals, as Belgium, Denmark, Holland, Norway, Yugoslavia, and other countries learned only too sorrowfully. Therefore, Germany could not at that time legitimately claim any reciprocal observation by neutrals of their legal duties as neutrals. This is especially true in view of the fact that the neutral in question, the United States of America, was at that time (1940) clearly in imminent and serious danger, by virtue of Hitler's publicized program of world aggression. The instinct of self-preservation, itself, called for the American recourse to the elementary right of anticipatory self-defense in a situation in which belated defense, according to the textbook rules of the strictest technical neutrality, would very probably have proved fatal both to England and the United States and therefore to the cause of international law itself. (On the policy of "fool-proof neutrality," see Coudert, "International Law and American Policy During the Last Thirty-Five Years," 1941, 35 *A. J. Int. L.* 429). One has only to go back to Grotius, in 1625, to see clearly the legality of the action of the United States in 1940: "It is the duty of those who stand apart from a war to do nothing which may strengthen the side whose cause is unjust, or which may hinder the movements of him who is carrying on a just war, and, in a doubtful case, to act alike to both sides . . ." Grotius, *De Jure Belli et Pacis, Bk. III. c. XVII, § III, cl. I.* Incidentally, "it has been noted that during the war between Russia and Japan in 1904 and 1905, the German Government permitted the sale to Russia of torpedo boats and also of ocean liners belonging to its auxiliary navy. (See Wheaton's *International Law*, 6th ed. (Keith), Vol. 2, p. 977.") 39 *Ops. Att'y Gen.*, 1940, 484, 496.

Finally, there is no valid reason to believe that the United States of America would not be willing to submit the question of its alleged violation of neutrality by the destroyer deal (which, incidentally, cannot reasonably be denominated "aggressive war") to an international tribunal for adjudication.

A NOTE ON THE TYPE

The text of this book is set in Caledonia, a Linotype face designed by W. A. Dwiggins, the man responsible for so much that is good in contemporary book design and typography. Caledonia belongs to the family of printing types called "modern face" by printers—a term used to mark the change in style of type-letters that occurred about 1800. It has all the hard-working feet-on-the-ground qualities of the Scotch Modern face plus the liveliness and grace that is integral in every Dwiggins "product" whether it be a simple catalogue cover or an almost human puppet.

The book was composed, printed, and bound by H. Wolff, New York.